HEY ROCKY, WHO TOOK NORTHERN ONTARIO?

JAMES R. BEAR

HEY ROCKY, WHO TOOK NORTHERN ONTARIO?

James R. Stevens
Box 23, R.R. 13,
Thunder Bay, Ontario,
Canada P7B 5E4
jstevens@tbaytel.net

Note for Librarians: A cataloguing record for this book is available from Library and Archives Canada at www.collectionscanada.ca/amicus/index-e.html
ISBN 1-4120-9456-9

PUBLISHING™
Offices in Canada, USA, Ireland and UK

Book sales for North America and international:
Trafford Publishing, 6E–2333 Government St.,
Victoria, BC V8T 4P4 CANADA
phone 250 383 6864 (toll-free 1 888 232 4444)
fax 250 383 6804; email to orders@trafford.com
Book sales in Europe:
Trafford Publishing (UK) Limited, 9 Park End Street, 2nd Floor
Oxford, UK OX1 1HH UNITED KINGDOM
phone +44 (0)1865 722 113 (local rate 0845 230 9601)
facsimile +44 (0)1865 722 868; info.uk@trafford.com
Order online at:
trafford.com/06-1211

10 9 8 7 6 5 4 3 2 1

Publications of James R. Stevens

A-Too-Soo-Ka'-Nan (Stories)
by James R. Stevens, Indian Education Series, Volume 8 Confederation College, Thunder Bay, 1970

The Sandy Lake Trilogy:
Sacred Legends of The Sandy Lake Cree
illustrated by Carl Ray, McClelland & Stewart, Toronto, 1971

Legends From The Forest
by Chief Thomas Fiddler-edited by James R. Stevens, Penumbra Press, Moonbeam, Ontario, 1985

Killing The Shamen
by Chief Thomas Fiddler & James R. Stevens, Penumbra Press, Moonbeam, Ontario, 1984

*

Great Leader of The Ojibway
by James Redsky-edited and introduction by James R. Stevens, McClelland & Stewart, Toronto, 1972

Recollections of An Assinaboine Chief
by Dan Kennedy-edited and introduction by James R. Stevens, McClelland & Stewart, Toronto, 1973

Paddy Wilson's Gold Fever
by James R. Stevens, Upland Pedlars Press, Thunder Bay, 1976

Phillip Neault, Pioneer
by Mae Carroll-edited and introduction by James R. Stevens, illustrated by Ernest Adams, Upland Pedlars Press, Thunder Bay, 1976

Sacred Legends
by James R. Stevens-illustrated by Carl Ray, Penumbra Press, Ottawa, 1995

Roy Thomas: The Spirit of Ahnisnabae Art
By James R. Stevens, Ahnisnabae Art, Thunder Bay 2002

*

The Passenger Plane That Went To War Series:
Searching For The Hudson Bombers: Lads, Love and Death in World War Two
by James R. Stevens, Trafford, Victoria BC, 2004

The Maw: Searching For The Hudson Bombers
by James R. Stevens, Trafford, Victoria BC, 2005

*

Hey Rocky, Who Took Northern Ontario; The Book Ontario's Politicians
Don't Want You To Read
by James R. (Bear) Stevens, Trafford, Victoria, BC 2006

Acknowledgements

The author wishes to express his appreciation to the many citizens of northern Ontario listed in the pages of this book who have expressed their concerns on the many devastating social and economic issues that have impacted their lives. These expressions of dismay with an alien city state government range from a Grade nine student to mill workers and university professors across the great northwest.

In the preparation of this book many have assisted in various ways. They are Gerald McEachern, Britten J. Barten, Shirley Stevens, Sue De Weese, Russell Evans, my wife Karen Niemi-Stevens, Raymond Furlotte, Doug and Cindy De Guiseppe, Lorne D. Clark, David Christie and Gilbert Labine.

James R. Stevens
Thunder Bay, Ontario

CONTENTS

HEY ROCKY, WHO TOOK NORTHERN ONTARIO?

A NORTH-SOUTH STORY OF OUR TIME

Once in a very present sad time there were a Bear people living in a land full of beautiful lakes, rivers and tall trees up in the North Country of a place called Ontarario. These Bears, Bearettes and their handsome cubs were harshly ruled by a distant land full of Raccoon people from a place way down in the southeast called Tarana and the GTA-Greater Tarana Area. Northern Bears as a group of subjected critters had all the usual complaints. They were being taxed unfairly without representation. They had no real control over their local affairs. Their language and cultural habits were not respected. After a century of this treatment the Bears were still colonists in their own forests. They were bound to a far-off power. Ordinary Bear folks shouted for justice. Their grieving voices went unheard. Their local politicians were losers not leaders. The Raccoons from the land far away were over bearing Imperialists who smugly governed them as Great Lords controlling their economy and social activities. Ordinary Bear folks were naturally upset with their near stateless condition. They had been made helpless and ineffective in their own land.

The dreaded condition of the Bears up in North Country had occurred years past when Rocky the Raccoon from little old Ontarario took Princess Betty Bearette as his woman. Betty did not really want to marry Rocky. Their initial meeting was shaky. Rocky met her at a debutante's ball put on

1

by the Government of Canada. Rocky knew this bear babe had a terrific dowry that included gold, billions of trees, water power galore, silver, copper, nickel, lead, zinc and more. The charming Rocky said to Betty, "Did it hurt when you fell from heaven?" Betty who was quite a forward bearette looked little black masked Rocky over with a smirk then she replied, "I'd like to screw your brains out, Rocky, but it appears someone has already beat me to it."

Nevertheless the Government of Canada issued a wedding certificate in an arranged marriage. It was never to be much of a relationship and it got worse as time went on. Most of their once well-treed Bear lands were stolen from them by Rocky Raccoon and his ilk. Raccoons took their profits and handed back stale beans to the Bears. They told the Bears, "Be happy. We don't want to hear Bruins sniveling." Bears were angry and dismayed. This is their story, the story of the unhappy Bear People, their leaders and the Raccoon politicians who thwarted every demand made by the good Bears and the Bearettes in the northern forests.

THE BEARS, BEARETTES, RACCOONS & OTHER POLITICAL CRITTERS

Aircan, David, Mayor- (Affiliation unclear)

Beardy, Bear Chief

Botchup, Kenny - Raccoon (Liberal)

Browndoff, Mayor - Bear

Bruin, Rodney-Bear (Entertainer)

Bucksaw, Kenny- (Beaver) ($)

Chumpsters-a Big Box store

Climahill, Ms-Bearette in Raccoon Land

Crass, Mayor Annie-Bearette

Doer, Garibaldi-King of the Buffaloes (NDP)

Evening, Ernie-ex King Raccoon (PC)

Fiddbar, Deputy Chief Alvine - Bear

Freddy the Eagle- President, Eagle in Bear Land

Grovel, Mitchell MPP-Raccoon (Liberal)

Guile, Don-Don of McDinty's Raccoons (Liberal)

Haaper, Stevey-Grizzly, King of Canada (PC)

Hampson, Hockey MPP-Bear in Raccoon Land (NDP)

Hardwoman, Maria, Reeve-Bearette

Harrassment, Mike-ex King Raccoon (PC)

Linnforpetesakes, Mayor-(Affiliation unclear)

Ling, Pat-President, Raccoonette

Lung, Peter-Bear, People Activist

Mansculvert, Pete-Doomscaster

McDinty, Galton-King Raccoon (Liberal)

McLoud, Linn-ex MPP, Raccoonette (Liberal)

McTree, Donald-Bear forester

Moroless, Billy-MPP, Raccoon (Liberal)

Opinion, Rickardo-Bear

Powerless, Mickey, Mayor-Bear

Ray, Right Wing, ex King Raccoon (NDP)

Rumsey, Rockey MPP-Monster of Trees, Critters & Lakes (Liberal)

Schmoozi-MP (Bear/Raccoon) (Liberal)

Soupland, Dougie- Basement writer/architect

Squeal, Alain-Raccooncaster

Sweet Sing, Harinder-MPP Monster of Roads (Liberal)

The Walnut-a Big Box store

Vallee, Noyodel - MP Raccoon (Liberal)

Wightly, Dunce - MPP, Raccoon, ex Monster of Energy, (Liberal)

Wily, William, ex King Raccoon (PC)

WHERE'S SIMON
THE BEAR WHEN YOU NEED HIM?

Our story starts in the long ago north when there was a very industrious bruin named Simon the Bear. He was one of the first Bears to build a road in the forests. The road made it much easier for Bears going out west to Buffalo and Grizzly country. Today part of this road is named after him and although Bear people often speak his name, few recall anything about him. It was 126 winters ago that Simon the Bear said:

"Ontario has no means of dealing adequately with these distant territories (i.e. the Northwest)–The true policy, in my opinion, would be to come to an arrangement with Ontario in which the whole of Algoma, including the new territory should be formed into a separate province."
(February 18, 1880, MP Algoma-Simon J. Dawson. 1878-1889 Independent/Conservative)

Simon the Bear did not get his way. Betty Bear and Rocky Raccoon were married anyway. Today North/Northwest Ontario, is land ruled by Raccoons from their city state parliament. They lord over a very, very large place. A land so large it would make several countries in an intelligent world. A century later in the huge North/Northwest of the Ontarario land, the Bear people exist in the wilderness almost forgotten by the Raccoons.

The belligerent, callous and ignorant years of policies from brain-challenged Raccoon politicians, from smoky cities south to Tarana, Ottawa, Niagara and Windsor-the smog horseshoe of Ontarario, precipitate this long untold story. From dens in a political wasteland that is Bear country-the North/Northwest-the brutal bare facts must be revealed.

Black Bears accuse Ontarario Raccoon parliamentarians that they operate in government policy and mental attitude, as if the huge province they are responsible for, ends somewhere south of a gleaming giant nickel at Sudbury. Many Bears think in the emptying northland that a divorce and a legal settlement with the Raccoons is in order.

Bruins in the N/NW and Raccoons in southern Ontarario have been incompatible for years so let's end the bitterness with this dominating insensitive smog smoking master called the Ontarario Raccoon Legislature. This is what many Bears of today think.

A divorce initiated by Northern Bears could be easy. Since most of the Raccoon people have long ago forgotten they are married to Bears and Bearettes through a provincial legislature, how could they miss the Bruins when they are gone? There will be no fighting over assets or bickering over who looks after the cubs on weekends simply because Raccoons just don't recall they were ever married in a hasty shot-gun 19th Century wedding to Bears in the first place. The long ago union when King Rocky of the Raccoons married child bride, Princess Betty Bearette was doomed to suffer abuse. The arranged marriage was set up by three colonials who had never seen a beaver in their lifetimes. Harrison, a lawyer and politician from west Tarana; Hincks, a seventy year old former Governor of Bermuda and British Guiana and Thornton, the British Minister in Washington decided every tree, rock and river from Sault Ste Marie west to the Winnipeg River and north to Hudson's Bay should belong to Rocky as the dowry from the Princess.

Rocky and the Raccoon people in Tarana and the southern corn country became the beneficiaries of this marriage. In the end, Ontario's predominance of Liberal MP's in Ottawa certified the wedding arrangement. All the other Canadian MP's outside of Ontario thought it would be a poor marriage. They knew they were sending a child bride into eternal servitude. They were right a century ago and dead as they are now they are right today about the Province of Ontario. It's just too big for Tarana to govern. Unfortunately for black Bruins who live up in the North, it's not too big for them to neglect, exploit and gouge. For over a century Raccoons have profited mightily from their arranged marriage with Bear Country.

Today there are 103 elected parliamentarians in the Raccoon legislature in Tarana. The collective knowledge of the present 103 parliamentarians is far less than the few pages found in this irreverent story. Really, the bare case for a separate existence from the Raccoons might be a bit gruesome, but how can there be a divorce if northern Bruins don't tell their half blinded partners in far-away land that they are dummies in a totally incompatible union.

Perhaps, it is unwarranted to consider there is any merit in insulting the Raccoons because much to the consternation of their southern newspapers, The Tarana Star and the Tarana Globe & Mail half their constituents in the GTA don't read English anyway. Like, does anybody down there know Bears are up here?

"Say Bear, you live in Marathon? Isn't that near Sudbury? Tell me," the black masked guy from Kitchener says with a frown across his short forehead, "That's awful far away from civilization isn't it?" Of course this barrage from a foreigner, who is not interested anyway, does not deserve an answer. Bear with it, shake your head, save your breath and shrug.

But back to divorcing the ignoramus Rocky legislators from Kitchener, Scarberia, Niagara or London, it is clear Bears in the North/Northwest have to get their minds settled on this and since they are not much interested in politics anyway, they simply must shape up. Bruins are all passive and barely aggressive so electricity rates, mill closings, cow paths masquerading as highways, school closings, under funded everything, but especially colleges and universities, heating costs, ski hill shutdowns, (can you believe it, ski hill shutdowns) rail line closures, dumb game laws are in total, disastrous and need to be addressed. Solutions need to be found. The problem is Black Bears are all out snow machining, ice fishing, at hockey games, working (if they still have a job) or in the summer, swimming, fishing, boating, trying to grow tomatoes, golfing or swatting black flies. Too many Bear northerners in good old Ontarario don't know where they are in time and space. Is anybody paying attention to what is going on? Does anyone care the north/northwest is being-down-sized by the Raccoon's provincial and federal government policies. Do all Bears and their cubs have to move to Alberta? Is this the plan?

The Bears rail about the Raccoons but what about northern Bears? Just how many watts are in their light bulbs? Some quick self analysis is in order before Black Bears sign divorce papers.

The first thing Bear northerners must do is make a paradigm shift and take a good look at Ontarario and realize they have been for a century condi-

tioned to think upside down. It is time for the northern Bears to stop standing on their ball capped bare heads!

A BEAR'S VIEW FROM THE NORTH

DO NOT TURN THIS PAGE UPSIDE DOWN-this action will indicate how whacked your brain is!

It's a fact. Bears have been conditioned to look at Ontario as if they have been skating around on their noggins. Bear cubs in their geography lessons have been oriented with maps that are simply propaganda. An old Bear elder has observed that maps are not the territory and how true this is.

This map is the proper view southeast from the north. Get your mind right when you consider the huge province of Ontarario. This is a map right side up for Bears. And thinking of maps-how do we like those Raccoon Ontarario upside down road maps that are dominated by southern Ontario and have a little square on the back side of Northern Ontario giving the impression that Bear Country is about 100 kilometers miles wide. In the

9

21st Century it is time for Bears to get a grip about where they actually are in Canada.

The late great Simon The Bear

GEOGRAPHY & DEMOCRACY

MINNESOTA WISCONSIN MICHIGAN OHIO PENNSYLVANIA NEW YORK

ONTARARIO

Bear problems with the Raccoons began long long ago when Rocky force marched Betty the Bearette Princess to the altar and these irreconcilable issues are still strangling the health of the North/Northwest Colony in the so sad present day.

"The result of the independent member system is easily seen in the manner in which the District has been passed over as a nonentity in the redistribution of the increased representation of Ontario."
(The Weekly Herald & Mining Journal-Prince Arthur's Landing, May 20, 1882.)

Have Bears ever noticed that when you-a Bear politician- are making that trip of obeisance to the ultimate halls of power in Tarana or Ottawa from Kenora, Red Lake, Fort Frances, Greenstone or Thunder Bay to beg for your grant or to get a road paved after fifteen years of use that you pass over the American states of Minnesota, Wisconsin, Michigan, Pennsylvania, Ohio and New York? That is six units of democratic governance on the American side. You have to admit the Eagle Yankee folks like to take some responsibility for their own affairs. The Yankees were able to create in the evolution of their country the States of North and South Carolina, a North

11

and South Dakota.On the Canuck side there is no Province of Northern Ontario. The only city in Ontario named north is North Bay. These inhabitants are so far south, Bears wonder why it is not called South Bay. In Canada, citizens have ended up with one sprawling ungovernable Ontario where governmental power is concentrated in a 350 mile curve around little Lake Ontario. This concentration of political power in the GTA is tyranny. Many northern Bruins realize this fact.

Black Bruins often ask themselves what happened in Canadian history to create a political state that is larger than several countries in Europe. Well, blame that old whisky drinking Tory, Sir John A. Macdonald. He took the first step to set-up Rocky's marriage to the very appealing Bearette Princess in the north. She was one wealthy gal. Macdonald made certain that political power in the east would never be democratized by representative political power in the northwestern part of what would become Ontario. Macdonald created the Boundaries Commission in 1878. Old farmer Macdonald was not a chap who could count beyond 10. There would be 10 provinces, no more, because that would mean 11 provinces, a number that would unmanageable for old Farmer Mac in the new country of Canada.

"If the Canadian Nation exists in defiance of the rules of logic, the Thunder Bay area may be taken to represent the dubious middle," wrote Bear Professor Elizabeth Arthur from her intelligent perspective at Lakehead University in 1973. Further, Arthur wrote in her introduction to 'Thunder Bay District 1821-1892', "questions concerning the inter-provincial boundary [between Manitoba & Ontario resulted in] discussion among residents of Thunder Bay as to which, if either, province they would prefer. The idea of being separate from both – had obvious attraction,"

Of course northern Ontario Bears in the 19th century had no say in the marriage arrangement to Rocky and his Raccoons in the east. Only the many protestations by MP Simon the Bear Dawson slowed the marriage and the usurping of Algoma and the northwest.

The Ontario Raccoon Legislature complained:

"The Lieutenant Governor expressed regret that the Federal authorities continue to dispute the title of the Province to the northerly and westerly portions of the Province."

Kenora Bears, at Rat Portage, who thought they were part of Buffalo country, Manitoba, were forthright in their hostility to the far-off Ontario

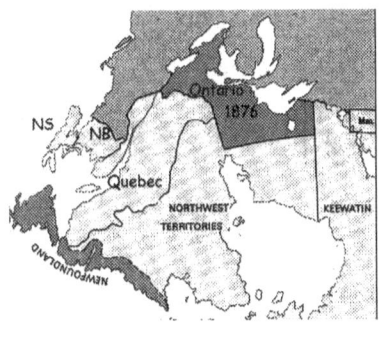

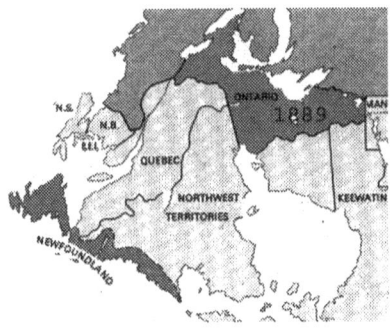

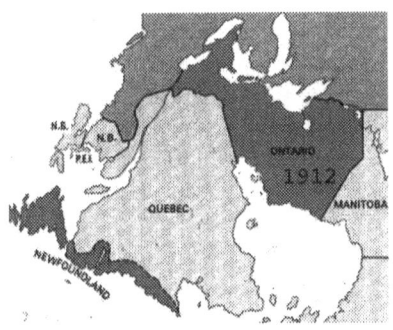

Legislature.

"Ontario will have a division court held in Rat Portage next month. Manitoba has one this month. The late incorporation under Manitoba appears to have 'riled' Oliver Mowat and he intends to subdue this territory if it takes two armies to do it. The first-an army of officials-has been dispatched, the second will probably be the Queen's Own Rifles, who will likely have orders to shoot down every mother's son of them who dares to rebel. The best thing the people can do when Mowat's soldiers come is to take them up the lake a few miles and then cut them adrift. They would never get back." (Rat Portage Progress Reported in The Herald Sep 23 1882)

By 1912, as you can see from the maps, Rocky and the eastern Raccoons had the great northwest all sewn up-the wedding certificate was signed-and from the outset the plan has been to milk Princess Bearette's north country dowry for all it is worth in timber, gold, silver, base metals, palladium, diamonds (these days), hydro-electric power, manpower, as a transportation corridor both by water and substandard highways to western markets. Milk the north and put as little back in the area as possible. Treat the area as a colony of dimwitted Black Bears who won't quite catch on if 2 cent candy canes are put on their trees at

Christmas.

The North/Northwest of Ontario instead of joining the west where it has many economic ties, or becoming the 11th province, was to become the outhouse of the Raccoon East! The area is a crapper in the back forty only to be given some attention if a particular Raccoon party in a close election might need a seat or two for political dominance in the remote urban brained centres of Tarana or Ottawa.

This geographical centre piece, Bear Country in the Canadian Confederation, has never placed a Premier in Tarana or a Prime Minister in Ottawa. Pay attention NDP Hockey Hamson-no Bear politician can ever be the Premier of Ontarario. Just ask ex Raccoon Liberal Leader Linn McLoud who tried and after she lost an election to PC Mike Harrassment was dumped out of politics like week old soap. As far as belonging to the political party in power there have not been effective politicians in the northwest since the late Robert Andras MP (Liberal) and Leo Burnyay MPP (Conservative). These two Bruins, however, were just buffers against stupidity coming from the east not real solutions to northern disenfranchisement.

So, there Black Bears have it-a Raccoon Ontario of the present- for now and forever unless some political force arises in the North/Northwest to dissolve a shotgun wedding to the urban east. How sweet or sour this union is for Bear northerners to decide. If only they can get their own politicians and corporate leaders out of a sterile bed with the Raccoons in Tarana. It is time for Northern municipalities and their Chambers of Commerce to bear-up, hold some plebiscites-join Manitoba-create a new province-or stay with the black masked corn eating raccoons in the southeast and suffer abusive treatment forever.

Whether leaving the urban south can ever happen or not is the question. It would involve another paradigm shift and this could be a huge mental problem for northern Black Bear politicians, many of whom think there is merit in being subjects of the Raccoons. Hell, these Bear politicians would have to think outside their cozy dens. It might be just too much for some of them to contemplate. Bear leaders of the present would have to cast away their defeatist mentalities and juvenile colonial reverence for that great centre of alien power, Raccoon infested Tarana.

The bottom line for shucking off Tarana as a master is, really, there is no choice. It is either create a Bear Province, adhere to Buffalo Manitoba or face an even gloomier Raccoon future than exists now. The future under the present system of non-representative government is that in 25 years there

14

will hardly be any Bears living in the N/NW. Observe the out-migration from the half depleted Bear forests. There are two Bear families in the neighborhood that have twenty something children. In one family of four, 50% are gone one to BC, the other to Korea. In the second family of three cubs, all three are in BC, 100% gone and the parents will follow the cubs as soon as they retread. This info is just anecdotal. Take a look at the 2001 report "Youth Out-migration in Northern Ontario" that is based on 2001 census statistics. It states, "The rate of youth out-migration is extremely high," and "has increased substantially since 1996." The overall rate of cubs gone from their northern communities is 18.5%. For Timmins the rate was 20.1%, Sault Ste Marie 24.8% and Thunder Bay 12.4%. One can expect these high rates to sky rocket after the extensive shutdowns and lay-offs in 2005-2006.

What does this mean for parents? It means from now on they will chat with their cubs by email. They will not make it back from BC or Tarana or Korea for your birthday Mom or be at the table at Christmas. You will have a difficult time seeing your grandcubs. If they do come the stay will be short. Like many Bruin parents in the north you will seriously consider moving to the area where the cubs live once you retread. But, hey!, they have Thunder Bay Days and Sault Days in BC already.

As for northern Ontario Bear Communities the word to get used to is, SHRINK.

The Town of Nipigon, Ontario in 2050

Okay, we are just bearing you here. This is the hub of Nipigon at the coming of the CPR. On the river is the long ago gone HBC Red Rock House south of the present marina. In 2006 the hub of the struggling village of Nipigon is a series of many empty stores.

CORN EATERS FROM A DIFFERENT CULTURE

It is an ongoing truth that folks from a different culture living in a different environment have a difficult time understanding others belonging to far-away-lands. Raccoons in their southern corn fields and in the walls of houses in the city of Tarana don't understand the aspirations of Bears in the bush and never will.

"The Ontario government seems to have deemed it right and proper to treat us with injustice, not withstanding we have the largest constituency in the province, and one from which a very heavy provincial revenue is derived." (The Weekly Herald & Lake Superior Mining Journal-Prince Arthur's Landing, June 8, 1881.)

Just to give you an example of this difference of cultural perspective between northern Bears and southern Raccoons here is a story.

NDPer Hockey Hampson of Rainy River country after much negotiation with the fastidious Don of Liberal Staff in Queens Park, Don Guile (the grad from Port Arthur Collegiate Institute-ho-ho) is allowed to talk to Premier King Raccoon Galton McDinty. Hockey is concerned that Galton just doesn't have a feel for the north, the beauty and grandeur of the place, the fresh air, the rivers and rapids, the fishing and so on. Hockey invites Galton to come to Fort Frances on a no public relations camping trip. It will be a fun outing with just the two of them. Galton is intrigued; he has never been on a camping trip. They negotiate, what kind of Scotch would they buy etc. So Galton and Hockey go out in the Rainy River country and set up camp, lay out their fishing rods for the next day's adventure. They drink their scotch and commiserate on how they are on opposite sides of the Raccoon house, but they are really friends in spite of their many differences. They tuck in their sleeping bags and fall asleep. In the middle of the night Hockey wakes up. He nudges Galton awake.

"Galton, take a look around and tell me what you observe." Galton sits up and looks up..

"Oh my God," he says, "look at the millions and millions of stars, that's amazing."

"What do you deduce from that observation," Hockey asks.

Galton goes intellectual, "Well, astronomically it tells me there are millions of galaxies and many, many planets out there to explore in the future.

I know he needs a shave that's why I'm drinking alcool!

18

Astrologically, I see that Saturn is in Leo, this might be propitious for my sun sign. Meteorologically, I think we'll have great weather tomorrow. Theologically, I can see that God is all powerful and humans are insignificant in his realm."

"No, No, No," Hockey instructs, "you have missed the essential point again, Galton, a black bear has stolen our tent."

Black Bears in the wilderness ask; just who are these Raccoon parliamentarians from Southern Ontario and the GTA who represent not only their own little political ridings as a responsibility, but supposedly the whole of big Ontario. How do far-off Bear Northerners describe them? One very important fact is these folks from their smoggy country live a vastly different culture. Those folks in the south are Raccoon People. When the unknown north of Ontario departs for real political representation and economic times, one predicts a reorientation of southern symbols: the Raccoon will be the official provincial animal for the GTA and the 10 million there because there are just about as many of these black masked bandits in Tarana as there are humans. So, if these humans are the Raccoon People in the south, who are the northerners in the bush? The answer is easy; Black Bear people.

Northern humans did not want to be known as the Black Bear people. Those black-masked Raccoon People forced it on us when their handicapped golfing Premier Mike Harrasment from south, North Bay changed the MNR Law-no hunting spring bears. Folks in the bush wanted to be the Black Fly people and they were the Black Fly people but not anymore. Northerners have almost as many bears now as black flies. There are bears everywhere. It is estimated there are over 100,000 black bears in the north for the 246,000 or so people living here. The bears seem intent on equalizing their numbers.

In the north, you can't even take a black bag from your house to the garbage bin without a black bear swiping the black bag out of your hand. In the northern district of Red Lake, Ontario, there are bruins everywhere. One guy reports he shot 17 bears in the summer of 2005. Others, taking a less drastic approach, throw cherry bombs at the bears. Explosions sound for miles. It's tricky being Black Bear people. Now, King Raccoon Galton McDinty and his smogged up parliamentarians tell northerners they have to learn to understand black bears. Open a dialogue with them when they are shitting on your lawn. Don't overreact when a bear is carrying your child down the laneway. Call a social worker on an 888 number in Louisiana for a consultation. (Actually, the call goes to a part time 'BearWise' worker in

Sault Ste Marie.) Like it or not, northerners are now the Black Bear people for better and sometimes worse. This story won't even mention the $40,000,000.00 loss to the economy up here in no-where Ontario. Not that northerners ever shot many black bears but our American friends loved to come up here and get their bears. It was a rite of manhood for those Eagle Yanks. They didn't have any bears left down there. Daniel Rac Boone shot them all. So up north they came and bush people collected their cash.

Northerners have long known it can be dangerous to go after bears. People in the north, sometimes to their own detriment believe in those phrases, bear with it, bear down, bear up, bear balls and bear ass. And Bear folks present status in the province could be described as barely existing. Anyway, northerners know you have to be careful going after bruins.

Take this recent case: At Sault Ste Marie, Louis Manickley and Dave Plant are out on the tug, 'Peck' owned by their boss, Louey Trempe. They are coming down the Sault River on a glorious clear night and they see a bear swimming across the river ahead of them. They race the tug up to the bear and start dispatching him with axes. These mariners then lowered their punt into the river to retrieve the bear. Holding the punt to the Peck with lines Manickley, Plant and another crew mate get into the punt and grab the bear and try to pull it aboard. It's big. The ropes on the punt get fouled and the weight of the bear and the three men is just too much and the punt turns over. Dave Plant and Manickley are then swept away in the current with the dead bear. And very soon, not only is there a dead bear there are two dead bear-killers. The question around the docks for quite awhile was, how many humans does it take to kill a swimming bear: two dead humans for one dead bear. This is poor odds for bear hunting. By the way, this happened in June of 1882. It is suspected that the Peck was an American tug.

The fact is northerners have a healthy respect for black bears. North people just have to understand the Raccoon people have a different culture and so far we have just adjusted grumpily to their many eccentricities. The Raccoons of the south believe black bears are just a whole bunch of related by-blood Winnie The Poo's sashaying on the streets in the north. They have a very urban attitude about bears. Take the urban-brained visitor who was feeding a Winnie some Smarties while his film director companion had the camcorder running. The visitor ran out of Smarties and Winnie was insulted so he/she smacked the guy a good one for a few stitches and torn clothing. This lover of Winnie immediately developed a hatred of Winnie and all bears. Winnie was now a beast. The guy wanted Winnie hunted down. At first, officers from MNR were sympathetic because the guy was pretty beat-up. When the film director mentioned they had a video of this unprovoked attack the MNR officials asked to see it and they twisted their intestines laughing at the climax. The moral of the event is if you are going to feed Winnie, Smarties, MNR says the minimum amount to satisfy him is 100 pounds of those colored chocolate pellets.

There are more ingrained cultural differences between northerners and southerners than love for the Winnies. Raccoons are nuclear people. Possibly it sounds better if we say they are Atomic People! Boy, do they love their reactors-the billions they have spent to keep their lights on all night. Ever drive in Southern Ontario at night? There are lights everywhere. They never shut them off because they are all afraid of the dark-even in the daytime. The Raccoons in the legislature are posed to spend another $35-40 Billion on nuclear upgrade and expansion so all those air conditioners in Tarana will keep operative. Of course, the North/Northwest people- Black Bear folks-are to be the beneficiaries of this. They are to get the toxic waste that lasts so many life times one must say that our grandcubs to the 100th power will be dealing with the stuff. But hey, all 11 jobs gained by the north will make it all worthwhile. Not really. Humans in the north are Water People, not Nuclear People. They like lights, too, although they don't feel compelled to eradicate the night because it interferes with the black bears. They like the dark. They see better in the dark. It's easier for the bruins to find the bird feeder, trash, the apple trees or your dog in the dark.

Another thing about southern culture-they think it is perfectly normal to be driving in 10 lanes of traffic at 130 clicks and sit in the exhaust of a million vehicles for an hour or so on their way to and from work. They have a rush hour all day long. When Bears visit the distant smog and drive the 401 or 400 or QEW they are mostly scared shitless. Who in their right mind tailgates at 130 klicks while putting on their lipstick? Those black-masked Raccoon People do. By the way Bears, it is illegal to use your signal lights when you are changing lanes on the 401.

All this speed is normal if you are an atomic driven person from the GTA. This mad rush produces some interesting statistics in Raccoon Land. In the GTA there are 56,210 collisions a year, 2,085 pedestrians are whacked and 1,006 cyclists are nailed. The Tarana death rate is one person every 5 days. The 401 yearly death rate is around 850 people per year. (In northern terms this means every single person in Red Rock, Ontario would be dead in a 12 month period.) Many spend more time on the highway than a lot of long distance truckers and they love it. Public transportation in the south: that's a mode for losers, not happening people.

Yeah, we're tarring all the Raccoons with the same stick. We know there are good environmentally social conscious folks in the south, even a few who have traveled north of North Bay and got lost where there is only one highway. Those southerners are so environmentally conscious that's why they have a quadzillion tons of garbage they ship to Michigan and really, really, really expensive guns laws to keep people from being shot daily on Tarana's main streets. It's a different culture and these Raccoon People-with bony little black hands- rule the north like it is not even a part of the province of Ontario. Given the lack of representation and almost complete lack of influence of northern politicians-all 6 of them (5% of the seats) in the present 103 seat provincial legislature in distant Tarana; it is time for Black Bear people to wave good-bye to the Raccoon People-the Atomic People-the Smoggers of the alien southeast. Bear people want our lands, lakes, and forests back.

Believe it-Raccoon people will not miss Bears. They will not even know there is a new Bear Province in Canada or that Bears have joined the Buffalos in Manitoba. Why won't they miss the Bears? Why, they have their own daily colossal problems. Their garbage problem has been mentioned.

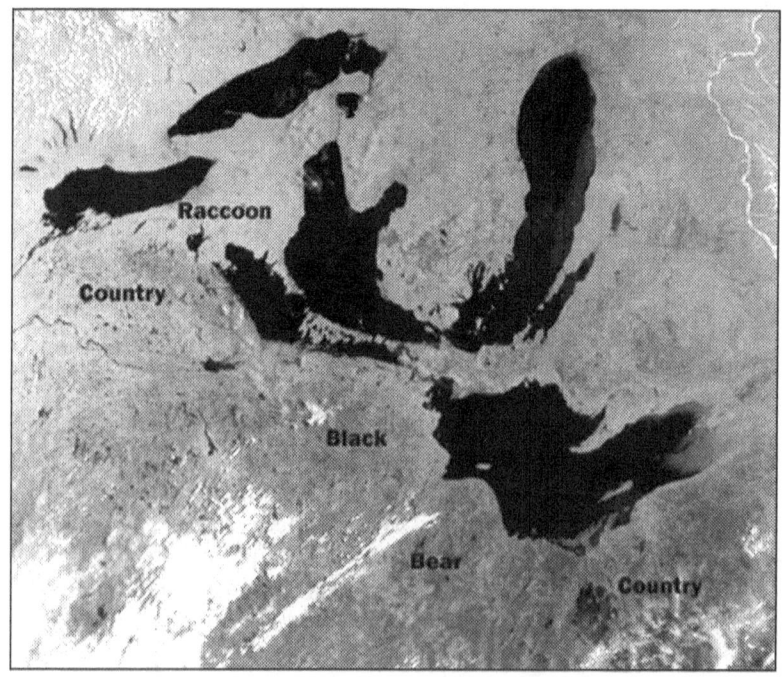

On a Raccoon personal level Tarana and the Golden Horseshoe is a place where you can make $150, 000.00 a year and can't find a place to live. As one Taranian says, "you spot an empty parking space and you are so happy it brings tears to your eyes." Raccoons have only a city view of their turf.

Northerners are invisible to southerners. Describing this fact in a different way, it is written: "Northern Ontario does not easily fit into the image most Canadians have of Ontario. Disparity between the north and south within Ontario is as great as the disparity between Ontario and the Atlantic provinces." It is true, not only for Canadians in general but, also for the southern Ontario Raccoons, they have no realization of Bear country. They will never know Bears are gone.

The epic point of this saucy attack on the well-suited Raccoons of the Ontario legislature is, that for Bears of all political stripes the idea of divorcing the south is essentially quite sound. It doesn't matter whether you are Green, Progressive Conservative, Liberal, NDP or a Druid. It doesn't matter if your parents came from Italy, Finland, Poland, Sweden, Scotland or southern Ontario, or are a First Nations person who has ancestors that date back 5000 years. If you are from the North/Northwest sitting in the wrong legislature, playing on the wrong ball field, dancing to the wrong music, adhering to the wrong rules and associating with a remote parliament that represents almost none of the aspirations of your communities and the future of your man cubs, you have to ask yourself, why not take responsibility for yourself? Bear-up Bear people!

The urban legislature in Tarana is foreign territory. The Golden Horseshoe politicians only represent their own culture and rightly so. That culture is urban and urban-brained. There are people there that have not seen the stars for years. They could not tell the difference between a partridge and a chicken. Their Raccoon children think retread hockey player Doug Gilmour still owns a milk making machine. These urbanites get up in the morning, walk down concrete, get in their cars, risk their lives in traffic and car fumes, go into an air conditioned building to look at computer screens, breathe recycled air, get in their cars, and hope on they way home they won't be shot at, get out of their cars walk on concrete and insulate themselves in their cubicles to watch doomscaster, Peter Mansculvert on TV. Many of them have not walked on grass since they moved to the city for economic survival years ago.

"Why would you want to live away up there?" a Raccoon southerner asks a northern Ontario relative. This question is a reflection of their disdain and ignorance for any person living north of Sudbury. Humble bears are polite in the north so they just shrug their hairy shoulders as if fate has dealt them a rotten hand. They don't want to offend, so they don't say, "Who in their right mind would want to live in this smutty, smog filled, elbow-knocking turf with 9 million dazed car racing maniacs driving on 10 lanes through a sea of concrete for 3 hours a day to get a pension if you survive a pile-up. Southerners just don't get it about the more relaxed qualities of northern living.

In the 1980's Right Wing Raccoon Ray and his NDP government transferred the Ontario Registrars Department and OSAP Student Loan Departments to Thunder Bay. Ray was trying to do Bears a good deed. All the Tarana civil servants had the opportunity to move north with their jobs. Of the 170 or so positions only about 5 Raccoons came north. The rest looked upon Thunder Bay as if this was a terrible banishment to a Communist gulag in Siberia!

The disconnect between the North/Northwest of Ontario is actually a natural one and this bare boned story considers that it would be natural for black bruins to break colonial ties with the ignoramus urban government and take charge of their own affairs. Or, at the very least, join the Buffalo people in Manitoba.

What goes on in Tarana often baffles the noggins of northern Bruins. On June 20, 2006, the Tarana Star-the Federal Liberal Party's marketing rag for the same-old same-old, reported that Dougie Soupland, the talented Vancouver basement writer/architect has been engaged to design a park that will overlook the Gardiner Expressway. Is this so all potential park goers can breathe the gas fumes rising like a cloud off the expressway, or have their hearing impaired from the noise emanating from below? Soupland is quoted, saying that he wants to build a "killer toboggan run" on the site. Of course the run will have a hell of a large snow making machine or artificial ice maker for the 60 days of winter in Tarana when the thermometer is well above 5c. A killer toboggan run, what a joke. How long is it going to be 200 metres? You want a killer toboggan run, Dougie, go north from Sault Ste Marie and you could built a toboggan run five miles long with enough twists and turns to spin your stomach a hundred times. But, then what, Sault Ste Marie? How would Raccoons from Tarana ever find their way that far north? They don't have much corn stored in the Sault.

It is difficult to underestimate just how different a culture there is in the south of Ontario. These differences get brought home in amusing ways. Here's a little true joke that gives an illustration.

Two OPP officers east of White River are sitting in their cruiser on a dark winter night sipping their coffees. A car comes down the lonely highway. Its right head light is hanging straight downward shining on the road. The windshield has a thousand cracks on the left side. The bumper is askew. The rearview mirror on the driver's door has been torn off and, to top it off the car is 15kmph over the speed limit. The cops look at each other and one cop says, "That car is a dangerous wreck!" The OPP guys turn on their red lights and give chase pulling the car over. They walk up to the car and a sixty year old Chinese/Canadian man from Markham rolls down his window. "What happened to your vehicle?" the cops ask. The man replies from a terrified face, "Big hairy munster jump on car, got to keep going."

The guy was making his first trip out of Markham since immigrating to Canada to go to a niece's wedding in Winnipeg. This may seem extreme but how many from the Golden Horseshoe have ever seen a live moose?

How many people from 416/905/519 ever find their way past North Bay? When these people go north they go to Buffalo.

Ever listen to CBC Radio Noon, 'Ontario Today' from Toronto or Ottawa? This program hosted by Alain Squeal, emanating from the urban south is like listening to a radio program from Jacksonville, Florida. It's just so alien for bear minds. The programs are like: What's wrong with the tulips on my brown lawn-the Gardening Phone In. Or, how can I solve my legal problem, my husband ran away with the paper girl. Or how do you fix a cat from doodling on the rug-Pet Behaviour. So, so exciting and relevant to northerners it just makes Bears want to change the station to a Jesus frequency to get something up to date. Think 'Ontario Today' could ever broadcast from Kenora or Timmins once a year. No way. No money. No inclination.

The other forms of media are no better. Take MacLeans magazine, the magazine, is so Tarana and urban. They give space to Pete Mansculvert and Barbara Amorous who are both as exciting to contemplate as wet cornflakes in butter milk. Thousands of jobs are lost in the North/Northwest and not a line. A secretary loses three of her children on their way to their grand mother's funeral on that cow path called the TransCanada Highway just before Christmas. Not a line. MacLeans is not connected to us in the same province. The point is all of the south, the legislature, the media, do not even faintly represent the Bears or their communities in the North/Northwest. They are just not interested in what goes on in the province and why should they? It's a matter of the urban market for their urban products and urban raccoon votes.

In Bear country every single decision in education, health, transportation, economics, manufacturing, every decision about anything that Bear politicians make is directed and controlled by the corn eating Raccoons. MP's MPP's, Mayors, Presidents, Reeves, Councilors, Bored members in Bear Country are deluded if they think they have any independent authority. The big political game with all the important rules set in the southeast are: they win, you lose. They take, you give. You give $5.00, they give .50 cents back. Be happy about this, Bear politicians? Download on the defenceless is the modus operendi from corn and smog country. Take the small Bear village of Pickle Lake with a population of 350 souls. Their policing costs have sky rocketed from $90 per household to $800 per household under a set in the Raccoon east formula, this is brilliant mathematics for the black masked robbers in the city state parliament, but a total bitch for the Bears. About the only thing a politician in the north/northwest can decide is whether to put up or take down is a stoplight and we're not even sure about this.

The question for Bears is, why should they be connected to these Raccoons with what must be the world's longest umbilical cord?

The Northern Ontario Building at the corner of Bay & Adelaide in down town Tarana pre-World War One. It was long, long ago vacated for lack of interest in the north.

Now, the North is so forgotten when the Raccoon people's civil servants in the Monster of Tourism put out a brochure on Ontario's Great Fall Drives they include nothing west of Thunder Bay. Rikardo Opinion recently blasted the distant Raccoon Ministry of Tourism for its winter brochure on tourist destinations which has virtually no representation of events north of Superior. Rikardo, (who has issued two opinions for every bear in the N/NW) asks, "is the McGinty government trying to impoverish the Northwest so we will welcome the economic benefits that come with being home to a radio active nuclear dumpsite?"

Furtman's book on Black Bears was published by Northwoods Press. It is an interesting read and worth while book.

Bears in the Northwest have to be lawyers to figure out the fishing laws set by MNR. That's why this couple looks so confused.

BANANA TURF LAND & ELECTRICITY

The Bear Colony in the big north of Ontario has suffered the pain of their hopeless status for a long time, too long a time as far as most Bruins with a brain believe.

"the injustice done our grand district in compelling her to have but one man representing her in parliament is obvious to the whole country. Here we have a stretch of country as great as all the rest of Ontario and resources more varied, and yet we have but one man to represent our mines, forests, fisheries, agriculture and manufacturing interests."
(The Herald, Prince Arthurs Landing, March 12, 1892)

Bear lands north and west of Sault Ste Marie were relegated to the status of banana turf-with no bananas even- in January 2006 when King Raccoon Galton McDinty's urban Liberals lost a bid that was something under a paltry $55 million for 196,000 square hectares (nearly a half million acres) of boreal forest and lakes in the Graham area of northwestern Ontario. With the sovereign ability to expropriate and pay the original owner, Abitibi-Consolidated, more than the winning bid of $55 M which came from an American forest company, Wagner Forest Management Ltd of Lyme, NH with a base in Minnesota, McDinty and his Golden Horseshoe Liberals sat on the toilet. So did the Ottawa Liberals. The three voiceless Ontario northern raccoon Liberals, Monster of Natural Resources, Rocky Rumsey, MPP Mitch Grovel, and MPP Billy Moroless all played the party line that the business community would have been miffed if the Province had intervened and expropriated in a private land transaction. Stupid! Stupid! Stupid! The issue was raised just who do these politicians represent, the people of Ontario or American business interests. The Yankee take-over is so anathema to northerners that the three MPP's should all have the word politician erased from their CV's.

Bruins in Ontario were outraged that this deal went down with McDinty's Golden Horseshoe crew sitting in the john. Even a Thunder Bay Chronicle Journal editorial called for expropriation-NOW! The northern out cry over this land sale was so strong that Grovel and Moroless changed their tunes and reported that Rocky Rumsey did not favour expropriation. Rumsey was going to humble on down to New Hampshire and have a talk with the Yankee Eagles. Like why? On the last day of January 2006, Rocky Rumsey reports that Wagner does not want to sell their property to MNR. Well, we guess not and Ontario will not expropriate. Don't those Raccoons have small brains, you bet.

So, what is the next thing coming down the pipe to insult black bared northerners. Possibly, it is the international bridge at Fort Frances that crosses to International Falls, Minnesota. The bridge owned by a paper company is for sale. Think MTO Tarana can afford to buy it? Not bloody likely. Do you think the Liberal Monster of Roads, Harinder Sweet Sing even knows where Fort Frances is in Ontario? Think Ontario or Fednor will even lend the money to the municipality of Fort Frances to buy the bridge. We'll have to see on this forthcoming sale. As for the business of owning this steel trestle, how can you possibly not make money on a toll-bridge. I guess the answer is, close it.

For the Tarana folks and the Golden Horseshoe MPP's this is a government that can think about spending $35 Billion for nuclear development in the next few years and then give up proprietary rights on a forest and lake area with all kinds of mid-sized hydro electric potential for future needs. It burns the pocketbook to think we have MPP's this shallow headed representing us.

At least the Liberal MP the Schmoozi could recognize the dismay of his constituents. So in the last week of the Federal Election of 2006 he suggested Ottawa could: (1.) ask for an environmental assessment on the land (2.)

have Industry Canada refuse to issue export licenses for logs going to the US from the property, and (3.) have the Federal Government expropriate the land involved. Good politics by the seventy-two year old Schmoozi, but you can bet nothing will ever come of these suggestions. Later, in an election debate the Schmoozi called the transaction "Unconscionable." It must be said for the Schmoozi, he knows how to recognize an issue and wait for it to go away. For he is the perfect Liberal politician; it takes the man a half hour to walk through a doorway but you would swear he was moving all the while. Nothing, you can bet the house, will come of Schmoozi's lamentation.

So now the enterprising Yankees own what could have at least been a lot of Galton Parks if Ontario's MNR had bid more than 50c an acre* (at the point of this writing nobody really knows what McDinty and Monster MNR Rocky Rumsey bid or if indeed there was a bid on this private land at all. Actually, one report stated they bid $40 million but then told Abitibi-Consolidated they would need a 100 years to pay them off.) The Yanks pay no stumpage fees on trees cut, can send the wood they harvest wherever they want, can legally keep out all the hunters and fishermen of Bear Country from their private property and just generally behave like Yankees. Lucky for them, peaceful Bears in the northwest are not extremist Muslims.

The sale of this nearly half million acres of course was hardly mentioned in the newspapers of the Golden Horseshoe. We are just too far away in the same province.

Just to give the folks in Raccoon country a view of the size of the new American territory in the Northwest, here's how it looks on a map of Perth County in south western Ontario.

News Flash-The People of Perth County Woke Up This Morning to Discover the McDinty Government has approved a sale of 80% of their County to a US Sod Company

PERTH COUNTY SOLD TO AMERICAN SOD COMPANY

It is rumored some of the people in Perth are actually miffed about this deal. (We must apologize to the people of Perth for this analogy because, in reality, ninety percent of the 10 lane Tarana people don't know where Perth County is in SW Ontario. So here's a hint for them, Perth County is in Stratford where they hold the Shakespearian Festival.)

What's the next economic insult from the Raccoon MPP's of the Golden Horseshoe, give away a billion dollars worth of Ontario's Lake Superior

Islands, shoreline and lake bottom for no secured significant investment from Parks Canada. Create a park inside an already park (The Great Lakes Heritage Coastline) with a bankrupt federal department like Parks Canada who can not obtain the resources to manage what they now control from coast to coast? There is no end to the garbage that is dumped from the southern legislature on the Bears and Bearettes of the N/NW in Ontario. Anything that will get urban votes in Raccoon lands is a go.

Then, there is the great electricity scam victimizing Bear homes and business. Electrical juice in bush land is generated by hydro electric power from several sites and coal-fired generating stations in Thunder Bay and Atikokan. Production costs are cheap. There is actually an oversupply that can not be sent south because there is a bottleneck in the power grid. In the south, other than Niagara Falls nuclear is a very big thing. I mean big-it's expensive. Money has been thrown at nuclear development for the Golden Horseshoe folks to the tune of giga-billions. The debt has to be paid and that debt is unloaded on the north. For Bears and Bearettes it is akin to paying off the neighbour's mortgage. The North/Northwest instead of having some of the cheapest power rates in Canada have the highest in Canada. Hydro costs in the N/NW exceed those in Manitoba by 250%. Why when bruins produce it so inexpensively. The answer is because the N/NW is being forced to pay down the Raccoon people's nuclear folly.

As Graham the Bear Sounder wrote in The Chronicle-Journal on October 11, 2005: "People in the Northwest pay debt for something that had virtually no benefits for the region." In the spring of 2006 it is estimated Bear residents in Sioux Lookout will face a rate increase of 17%, Atikokan, 7%, Terrace Bay, 16%, and The Fort, 5%.

The pulp and paper companies in the north have noticed they are paying off the southern love affair with nuclear power and their directors are shutting down mills up here faster than a bear cub can yell: "jack sprat."

There have been sane requests made by folks in the north to rectify the electrical rate scam. One policy would see Manitoba Hydro manage the Ontario West Electrical system and charge Manitoba rates for the sale of the juice to industry and homes on Bear turf. A second policy would see the Ontario West Electrical system manage its own rates independently from the nuclear Ontario East system. Because the two Electrical systems in Ontario are both managed by the Imperial political geniuses in Tarana these possible policies will never happen. Just ask the Raccoon gang member

Before the Raccoons went nuclear this is how it used to be in the north.

Billy Moroless (who supposedly represents his constituents), "Ontarians are building up a liability that's not showing up on their hydroelectricity bills." He speaks the raccoon people's party line like he lives in Scarberia. So let's get it straight in our bared heads people of the north. We are taxed through our electrical bills for a service never rendered. We are taxed for a nuclear electrical house we never built. We have this tax imposed upon us by a parliament that we have no voice in. We are powerless to change this because the N/NW of Ontario is a 21st century colony administered by the narcissistic Raccoon MPP's of the Golden Horseshoe.

The next McDinty move in the north that reeks with hypocrisy is the shut down of the coal generating station in the hard pressed community of Atikokan. Mayor Browndoff has a generating station that has a significant contribution to the thin Atikokan economy. Without seriously investigating the possibility of new technology (peat as fuel) to reduce emissions, the plant is to be closed and that's it. When Atikokan Bears hollered in protest they were referred to as "Neanderthals." Raccoon Monster of Energy, Dunce Wightly actually showed up in Atikokan offering no relief whatsoever. Despite the pleading from these northern citizens the end of this station is near. Atikokan will lose half its tax base and half of its jobs in 2007.

Are Black Bear people supposed to accept this like the good little bear colonists that they are?

Bears are told by these southern MPP's that they are Whiners. This is true. Bears are whiners. Look at the comments in the pages of this story. The thing is, it is time to stop whining and start walking away from a self imposed exile in Ontario.

Bear people who are members of a Chamber of Commerce, or an elected municipal leader, a car salesman, a teacher, an MPP, an MP, a paper machine operator, a carpenter need to start acting like they are not on some sort of political tranquilizer. It is time to start talks in Winnipeg. It is time to call a Northern/Northwest assembly. Just look at what the Iraqi people are going through to live in a democracy. If northerners start divorce proceedings with the south, Rocky and the Raccoons won't start shooting us, will they?

DOWNSIZING THE NORTH

Since the late seventies there has been deliberate government policy to downsize the Bear Country in the North/Northwest by both Federal and Provincial governments in Tarana and Ottawa. This perverse down-sizing has taken the form of withdrawal of services and financial commitment in transportation, communication, education, recreation, meteorological, business and just about any sector you can think of while maximizing revenue extraction from the area. Bear leaders have one migraine after another when they contemplate their fall into political and economic oblivion.

April 25, 2006 -Smooth Rock Falls: The Tembec pulp mill is idled. About 230 jobs will disappear in July.

April 15, 2006-Longlac: Buchanan Forest Products lays off 150 saw mill workers.

April, 2006-Northern Ontario: Northern Ontario Business reports that in 2005 the Ontario Ministry of Innovation & Research granted only 1.48% of innovation money to northern Ontario. On a per capita basis this represents less than 1/4 of the northern fair share.

April, 2006-Sault Ste Marie: The Federal Department of Fisheries & Oceans transfer 8 employees out of the Sault representing a loss of $14 million dollars in payroll to the local economy.

March 22, 2006-Atikokan: Quetico Centre, with over $2 Million in debt announces it's closing. The Centre, an educational retreat and learning facility has existed for 48 years. The facility buildings based on 50 acres at Eva Lake will be sold if a buyer can be found.

March 10, 2006-Dorion: Sturgeon Timber in the village of Dorion on Hwy # 17 declares bankruptcy laying off 70 employees.

February 20, 2006-Terrace Bay: Neenah Paper Mill down sized to idle lays off nearly 360 workers. Plant suspension is related to its union busting offer to 250 woodland workers who are on strike. Rumour is that the paper mill is for sale.

February 13, 2006-Hearst: Columbia Forest Products announces the Hearst Particle Board Plant will close April 14, 2006. About 76 employees will be without work.

February 11, 2006-Thunder Bay: CPR will close its freight container terminal on April 28. There will be a loss of 5 jobs.

February 09, 2006-Timmins: Tembec announces it is reducing costs at its Timmins Sawmill by giving lay-off slips to 19 people.

February 02, 2006-Sault Ste Marie: Eighty-eight percent of union members at St. Marys Paper vote affirmatively to take a 20% pay cut until April 30, 2009 hoping the plant can survive.

January 27, 2006-Thunder Bay: Bowater Incorporated announces the shut down of a kraft machine and the layoff of 20% of its workforce by May 1st. Job loss occurs for 280 workers.

January 17, 2006-Thunder Bay: Workers Coop store closes after a long history in Thunder Bay North. Six full time workers lose their jobs.

December 18, 2005-Thunder Bay: TB Source discloses that of "the 52,000 well paid jobs lost in Ontario over the past year most of them are in the northern part of the province."

December, 2005-Thunder Bay: Intercity Bingo closes after 15 years of operations. At one time fifty charities in Thunder Bay utilized the bingo hall for their organizations.

December 18, 2005-Dryden: Weyerhauser announces the closure of No. 1 paper machine, 80 employees will be let go. This is in addition to 30 wood room workers who received notice earlier.

December 16, 2005-Kenora: Abitibi Consolidated announces closing of their Kenora paper mill with a loss of 320 jobs

December 14, 2005-Greenstone: The Greenstone council declares there will be 12 jobs cut in the area, 2 in Nakina, 1 job in each of Longlac, Beardmore, Jellicoe, Caramat and Geraldton, with 5 jobs eradicated at the Geraldton Weather Station.

December 13, 2005-Marathon/Manitouwadge: Newmont Canada declares closure of the Golden Giant Mine by March 2006 with the loss of 170 jobs.

November 23, 2005-Thunder Bay: Cascades Fine Paper Plant will close on January 21, 2006 with the loss of nearly 400 jobs in the city.

November 13, 2005-Dryden: Weyerhauser announces the closure of its wood room in the Dryden plant resulting in the loss of 40 jobs.

November, 2005-Thunder Bay: Kings Stereo after nearly forty years of business in the city closes.

November, 2005-Thunder Bay: The Next Stop, an ice cream parlour in the CN rail station announces closure citing high rental costs.

October, 2005-Manitouwadge: Julien's Men's Wear closes after 37 years of business.

October, 2005-Thunder Bay: Regal Greetings & Gifts store in the city closes as a result of the company's bankruptcy.

September, 2005-Terrace Bay: The Terrace Council announces the closing of the Terrace Bay Airport citing high maintenance costs of $45,000 to

$55,000 per year.

September 22, 2005-Red Rock: Norampac Inc mothballs one of two production machines resulting in the loss of 85-90 jobs in the small Lake Superior community.

September 2005-Thunder Bay: Revenue from slot machines at Thunder Bay Charity Bingo fall 17% from a year earlier.

September 14, 2005- Marathon, Ontario: Citizens can not go to the municipal dump as it is infested with more than a dozen black bears.

August 30, 2005-Thunder Bay: Erco Worldwide announces it will close its Thunder Bay sodium chloride plant by April 2006 resulting in the disappearance of up to 30 full time employees. For two years Erco sought energy reduction costs-no deal. An estimated $2,000,000.00 will vanish out of the local economy.

August 25, 2005-Sioux Lookout: The Town Council raises municipal taxes by 12% due to Ontario's inadequate funding formula for northern communities.

July 3, 2005-Thunder Bay: Professor Bakhtiar Moazzami of Lakehead University, an expert on population demographics predicts Thunder Bay's population will fall to 94,000 by 2015. A previous estimate was gloomier than this.

May 2005-Thunder Bay: Tourism gurus at NOSTA report Americans crossing the Pigeon River Border are down by nearly 30%.

September, 2004-Thunder Bay: Human Resources and Skills Development Canada report the loss of 4,400 full-time jobs in the Northwestern Ontario Labour Force from a year earlier. Part time jobs over the same period suffered a 23.7% decline.

September, 2004-Thunder Bay: RMH Call Centre in the Eaton's Building closes ending jobs for 190 employees.

October 23, 2003-Thunder Bay: Smurfit-Stone Container Corporation on

Lakeshore Drive announces closure on November 14. Job loss equals 87 employees.

November, 2002-Thunder Bay: Shaw Bakery, one of the oldest surviving business's in the district (80 years) goes into receivership and ceases production of its bakery products.

June 2002-Toronto: A Provincial MPP Committee (mostly politicians from the Golden Horseshoe) tables its final report and recommends the closure of the Thunder Bay and Atikokan Coal-fired Generating Plants. As it evolves Atikokan will close and Thunder Bay will convert-at great expense-to natural gas necessitating a pipeline through the city.

March 2002-Ottawa: Statistics Canada reports Thunder Bay's population has declined by 4.1%, Sault Ste Marie by 6.9%, Schreiber by 19%, Terrace Bay by 16.1%, Greenstone by 13.3 %. In the northwest only Sioux Lookout has increased in population, a measly 3.3% since the last census in 1996.

June 2002-Thunder Bay: N.M. Paterson & Sons sell their seven grain and coal ships to Canada Steamship Lines and depart from the Great Lakes transportation scene after 87 years in business. Ten full and part time jobs are gone.

August 2002-Thunder Bay: Candy Mountain Ski Resort has over $400,000.00 in debt. It fails to find a buyer and closes. This leaves only two ski resorts in Thunder Bay, Mount Baldy and Loch Lomond.

December 2001-Port of Thunder Bay: grain shipments to terminals in 2001 dropped to a 33 year low. At least 300,000 tons of grain were diverted to Churchill, Manitoba supported by a federal financial assistance from the Liberal Crouton government in Ottawa. (The support to Churchill is strongly defended by M P Stunley Drumiske.) From a peak year in 1983 when 17,679,719 tonnes went through the port to 6,484,351 tonnes in 2001 indicates the drastic decline.

June 18, 2001-Kenora: Abitibi-Consolidated closes No. 8 Paper machine laying off 147 workers. Another 500 have job alterations.

1999-2001- Kapuskasing: The labor force drops from 5,303 to 4,415 jobs in a three year span.

1995-Thunder Bay: After 6000 volunteers helped successfully stage the 1995 Nordic Games the Big Thunder Ski Complex is closed for lack of Federal and Provincial funding. Several jobs are lost, but the more significant impact is on winter tourism.

1995-Thunder Bay: Northern Breweries (Dorans) on Algoma Street closes and property sold. No more Northern Ale or Kakabeka Cream Lager or Skidoo Oil for northerners.

1970-1995-Thunder Bay: The Port loses 10 grain elevators over this period. Smaller companies are purchased by large ones for their railcar quota's; efficency updates, shifting of world markets and large increases in the Great Lakes Seaway rates are all factors in closing the elevators. Saskatchewan Pool goes from 5 elevators to 1 and the workforce drops from 1200 to 120 employees.

January 1990-Sudbury-Thunder Bay: CPR passenger rail service from Sudbury into Thunder Bay is stopped without any public consultation. This ends a century of passenger service to the Lakehead. For convenience Lakehead and north shore residents now have to drive 220 kilometers to Armstrong, Ontario and stand by the side of the tracks to take a train east or west in Canada. Despite rather bland letters of support in 2004/5 from politicians-Botchcup, Moreless, Grovel and various local elected officials the service remains suspended.

January 1970-1990-CBQ Thunder Bay: By initiating a series of program changes over over a 20 year span CBC has eliminated 500 hours a year of regional communication between the residents of Northwestern Ontario.

1980-1995-Lake Superior: Lamb Island, Trowbridge, Porphyry, Battle Island, Slate Island Lighthouses at the western end of Lake Superior are automated putting seasonal lighthouse keepers out of work. The sites are abandoned and now serviced by helicopter. Cost savings are questionable.

1988-Kapuskasing: Penumbra Press of Kapuskasing/Moonbeam, Ontario, the northwest's only book publisher moves south to Waterloo, Ontario

1985-Shebandowan: Inco closes its Shebandowan Mine with the loss of 124 jobs resulting from the shutdown.

BRUIN VOICES IN THE WILDERNESS

Bear people in no where Ontario are drowning in the sweep of international globalization that has seen the arrival of city states like the Tarana GTA controlling vast areas of rural and forest hinterland and everyone who lives in these areas. Centralization of political power by virtue of citified population continues to demolish small communities everywhere. The cities are black energy holes blindly absorbing and obliterating the economies and the culture of rural citizens. In this story, Bear country-Northern Ontario is a case study on how a people might resist being diminished and swallowed. At the moment, Bruins are protesting with pleading voices for courageous leaders to take them away from this destructive force driven by far-off and mostly corporate brained Raccoons from a completely different geography.

"If the threat to secede from the province finally lights a fire –then lets get on with the job. When your fight is for survival every tool is an option. Politicians are an expendable commodity and leaders are in short supply."
Mike Mosley, Fort Frances, Ontario

"We have some great MPPs up here who are spinning their wheels in their

own parties. A change is needed."
Larry Phillips, Thunder Bay, Ontario

"People in Queens Park need to understand that the pain of job loss in our communities is very real."
Michael Power, Geraldton, Ontario

"The 'True North' though not so strong and free any more from Sault Ste Marie to the Manitoba border"
Ann Ray, Terrace Bay, Ontario

"Now that the 2005 school closures are done, I'm still amazed how few have read between the lines, and seen the closures were not done by the school board alone, but by our less than competent Liberal liars."
Jeffrey Mark, Thunder Bay, Ontario

"Years down the road, trustees will be trying to figure out how to bring back neighbourhood schools when they find out students did benefit from smaller schools."
Rhonda Molly, Thunder Bay, Ontario

"Rural schools are a very important part of our lives and community and should never be closed. If I had my way there would be more of them not less."
Doug Thomas, Pass Lake, Ontario

"You will find an attitude of 'Who cares' from Toronto. And why should they care? Northwestern Ontario is hundreds of kilometers away."
Jon MacDonald, Schreiber, Ontario

"We would add 243,256 more people to Manitoba – which would give us somewhere in the range of 10-15 seats – we would be better represented in Winnipeg than we currently are in Toronto."
Adam J. Di Felice, Thunder Bay, Ontario

"The next Ontario election is set for October, 2007 – hopefully, enough voters will desert their automatic Liberal mind-set and get rid of this destructive party" Norm Knott, Thunder Bay, Ontario

"Wake-up Northern Ontario! – our Fiberal MPPs don't care about the North."
Robert Woito, Marathon, Ontario

"The Golden Horseshoe is out of touch with the rest of the province, especially Northwestern Ontario."
John de Bakker, Thunder Bay, Ontario

"There are options to cry-babies and hypocrites. Some Canadians are working to give all Canadians credible options to improved democracy."
Don McAlpine, Nipigon, Ontario

"You are ripping off the people here in this community and this region and it's time we did something about it."
Ian Angus, Thunder Bay, Ontario

"I do think that maybe we should look to the federal government, to form a new territory maybe the Northwestern Ontaritory."
Wesley Webb, Dryden, Ontario

"Since Kenora wants to join Manitoba, how about moving the line farther east to say about Wawa!"
Waltraud Bobrowich, Red Rock, Ontario

"Regional government won't work –It has to be approved by the government of Ontario and the last time I looked 10 or 12 votes doesn't trump 105."
Michael Power, Greenstone, Ontario

"It's time Mike Gravelle and Bill Mauro show common sense and a bit of backbone. Come on guys, stand up and let your voice be heard."
Wendell Panula, Thunder Bay, Ontario

"Unless Northwestern Ontario is able to exert greater control over its destiny it may end up as a 'have not' adjunct to a 'have' province."
Cliff Huber & Retired Teachers District 2, Kakabeka Falls, Ontario

"The policies that are critical to northern Ontario never seen to make front page. I really do feel a betrayal."
Silvio di Gregario, Thunder Bay, Ontario

"The provincial government is missing in action."
Anne Krassilowsky, Dryden, Ontario

"Minister David Ramsay's so called New Vision for the Forest Sector in Ontario may benefit multi-national corporations and politicians that undermine democracy for personal gain but certainly not for the people of Northern Ontario"
Al Simard, Kapuskasing, Ontario

"Dalton, don't come here, don't talk to us, stay where you are. You are a mediocre man doing a poor job wearing shoes you can't possibly fill. You don't have the right to stand in the presence of real men and real women with real values. You are persona non grata in OUR province."
Rick Lambert, Thunder Bay, Ontario

"It took – an electoral gun to the Liberals head, to get Paul Martin to notice the forestry crisis in Northern Ontario. Until now we've seen nothing but silence and indifference as mill town after mill town have gone down across the north. Where was the Liberal's strategy for Northern Ontario when plants went down in Dryden, Kenora, Thunder Bay, Red Rock, Opasetika and New Liskeard!"
Charlie Angus, Timmins, Ontario

"Northern Ontario industries are going to die a slow death."
John Roswell, Sault Ste Marie, Ontario

"Even to say now that it's time to implement solutions is ridiculous. We needed them implemented months ago."
Mary Long-Irwin, Thunder Bay, Ontario

"We are not 'cry babies' for lamenting economic devastation that has been inflicted on us. After all we are being forced by our own provincial government to engage in a brutal struggle for economic survival."
Denis Brown, Atikokan, Ontario

" The region's political leadership has been timid because it is part of an established system of centralized government from the south that depends on Queen's Park for favour."
Livio di Mateo, Thunder Bay, Ontario

"I personally feel that Northwestern Ontario is quite capable of becoming an autonomous province with a fully functioning administration. Do we want to stay with a province that will only continue to exploit and neglect us ."
Adam J. Di Felice, Thunder Bay, Ontario

"A lot of people criticize – saying we couldn't make it on our own. I say to them, we are already on our own, we just aren't officially recognized by the country as an independent territory, and allowed to govern ourselves."
Shannon Nyman, Dorion, Ontario

"Maybe it is time to have a conference to discuss the pros and cons of separation. God knows, we are not getting anything out of Southern Ontario other than 'a kick in the rear'."
Bill Bartley, Municipality of Shuniah, Ontario

"We will have to leave town. What else can you do? There just isn't any work in Thunder Bay. It's in bad shape nothing coming down the pike."
John Jones, Thunder Bay, Ontario

"If nothing is done to stop the destruction of this city, there will be no future for Thunder Bay."
Kiley Broughton, Thunder Bay, Ontario

"David Leskowski is correct when he says that the current government is allowing federal jobs of quality, advancement, opportunity and stability to leave Thunder Bay to areas such as Sudbury and Ottawa."
Helen Pilchta, Thunder Bay, Ontario

"How committed is this government to the north?"
Mike King, Terrace Bay, Ontario

"I refuse to cooperate with a government that ignores me and I refuse to cooperate with a spirit of complacency that would destroy us as surely as the neglect of Queens Park." Lynn Enge, Atikokan, Ontario

"I am compelled to express my outrage that our governments have let us sovereign taxpayers down –"
Rick Prior, Thunder Bay, Ontario

"It is my sincere hope that the issue of the sale of 1,900 square kilometers to an American lumber company will not just fade away like so many other problems that we have had thrust upon us by so many of our complacent and self-serving politicians and civil servants."
Mike Barbeau, Kaministiquia, Ontario

"The problem is, the southern Ontario political power base does not listen to us in the north. Just ask the people living in Atikokan or Terrace Bay if they feel that our politicians are listening to them."
John Kaplanis, Thunder Bay, Ontario

"With the recent loss of almost 1,000 jobs in the forestry sector and no manufacturing economy to speak of, it would appear that about 1,000 families will be moving to Alberta, Southern Ontario or one of the many other jurisdictions in this country that have taken the road to prosperity."
Ian Hobson MD, Thunder Bay

"Justice was not served in the City of Thunder Bay when we citizens voted for a Charity Casino that saw only 5% of its operations go to the local charitable organizations. By my standard of justice, this was injustice."
Caesar Squitti, Thunder Bay, Ontario

"If the type of rigid thinking so prevalent in the handling of small communities in Northern Ontario continues ... don't be surprised to hear of a "municipal bankruptcy!"
Chris Wray, Wawa, Ontario

"One cannot be blamed for the nagging feeling that Queens Park is making soothing noises to the region's political leaders while implementing other more sinister plans."
Livio Di Matteo, Thunder Bay, Ontario

"Right now I think we're stagnating."
Rebecca Johnson, Thunder Bay, Ontario

"Lets face reality the provincial government couldn't care less about the people of northern Ontario. Their idea of the north is North York."
Val- email posted on Tbsource.com

"I've got to say to this government, you'd better start taking people more seriously. I'll tell you the wrath you're going to see in the next provincial election, the voter anger toward this government on the issue of employment, will be something like you've never seen before. I caution this government that you've got a chance and you'd better take it. If you don't, you're going to be in trouble."
Gilles Bisson, Timmins, Ontario

The recent sale of a large tract of prime woodlands in Northwestern Ontario – highlights the disconnect that the MNR seemingly has to residents here in the North. This is just another example of our northern resources and heritage being pawned off by poor planning and political expediency."
Mike Plexman, Thunder Bay, Ontario

"Wow-another Liberal blunder! I cannot believe that our provincial government has let 1/2 million acres with many lakes and timber stands slip into American hands. I'm dumbfounded."
Robert W. Plouffe, Shebandowan, Ontario

"I am very angry that our federal government would allow the sale of private Abitibi forest to a US-based forest company. I believe that the federal government should immediately initiate a judicial review of this sale."
Dan Edmunds, Thunder Bay, Ontario

"I was shocked to see the front page headline 'Abitibi sells N.W.O. forest to U.S. firm'. –Along with mills and jobs we are losing money because our Liberal government continues to milk Thunder Bay through its 'charity casino' which has given peanuts to our civic government from the proceeds."
G. J. Poling, Thunder Bay, Ontario

[Open letter to Mike Gravelle MPP.] "Whether it's us here in Marathon, or the people of Atikokan, the reality is that your government is for Southern Ontario and not for us." Robert White, Marathon, Ontario

"The question to be asked is: Why do so many vote for the Liberals election after election when they have never done anything for this area, neither at the federal nor provincial level?"
Michael J. K. Robinson, Thunder Bay, Ontario

"I have profound concerns about the potential loss of local health services and the chaos in my workplace that will be caused by the Liberals' new Local Health Integration Networks (LHINs)"
Mary Bava, Thunder Bay, Ontario

"NW Ontario voting to separate can only bring good. We are dying – now. Lets scare our Liberal caretakers in Toronto and either receive our true worth or divorce these knuckleheads. "
Roger Welyki, Nolalu, Ontario

"If we are to survive, we must get out now! Separate from Southern Ontario and form our own province."
R.E. La Plant, Thunder Bay, Ontario

"Northern Ontario is in crisis mode but the government still choses to ignore the problems we face. Maybe it's time to consider joining Manitoba, or forming our own province. Drastic times call for drastic measures; and we can't afford to wait much longer for an uncaring government to come to our side."
Anna-email posted on Tbsource.com

"I am disturbed with the closing of the single parents program because of pulled funding from the government, with all it has done to build a better community."
Holly Loonskin, Thunder Bay, Ontario

'The closing of Haven House is a serious loss for Thunder Bay and especially the young people who found refuge there."
Allan Moon, Thunder Bay, Ontario

"Our option of staying here is not good. We're losing population and our industries are falling apart."
Tannis Drysdale, Fort Frances, Ontario

"My question is, Where is the public outcry? The silence is deafening. –They say it takes a village to raise a child. Three years ago when Haven House opened I quietly cheered."
Christine Sandford, Thunder Bay, Ontario

"I don't think I've ever read about such a great idea –that local MP Joe Comuzzi resign from the Liberal Caucus and sit with the Tories."
Adam Moir, Thunder Bay, Ontario

"If the power source and understanding of the region come from Manitoba then Mantario it must be. It's all bureaucratic paper shuffling. Becoming a Manitoba province has many advantages. When was the last time Ontario gave the Northwest an advantage?"
Judy Skidmore, Callander, Ontario

"As for Mr. Ramsay insinuating mill and bush workers are overpaid, I would say this to him. At least the mill or bush worker earns his paycheck, unlike you sir. – it is time for you to be severed from your job."
Jeff Hunter, Thunder Bay, Ontario

"Mr. Ramsay, you have lost any respect and confidence I may have had in you, and any hope of my (and likely other's) future vote. You need to resign from your position. Obviously you are way out of touch with real issues."
Len Day, Thunder Bay, Ontario

"Let us form our own government so that we can have a say in our future. Not some people 1,000 miles away. If not, we won't be able to live here much longer."
Bill Costello, Atikokan, Ontario

"We of Dryden along with all affected communities in Northern Ontario are suffering from the same indignity from Queens Park and must rally and some how think outside the traditional political box."
Joe Delaney, Dryden, Ontario

"The government is so detached from our situation in the North they can't even be bothered to send someone in person for us to talk to."
Larry Kadolph, Thunder Bay, Ontario

"The focus of our attention should be on our provincial government. The people and communities in Northern Ontario are as important as those in southern Ontario."
Charles Primeau, Longlac, Ontario

"I think a lot of people in our situation are stuck here whether they like it or not, because we can't sell our homes. You have to feel sorry for the younger people. I don't think there's a future here for anyone under 40."
John Vandergraff, Terrace Bay, Ontario

"Do we have a dearth of quality candidates or do we just have to vote dumb?"
J.F. Mills, Thunder Bay

"Neenah Paper expects us to go back 60 years in time by imposing a contract and not negotiating in good faith. This is why we are standing up now and are refusing to be brought down that low."
Rolly Couture, Longlac

"I am an employee of the Lakehead Board of Education and like others before me, I am now compelled to speak out. I am beginning to feel embarrassed to say I work for this board given the recent developments of their high school closure plan."
Name withheld for personal protection

"I am asking the board to please reconsider its decision and not close Port Arthur Collegiate Institute."
Chris Zaiser Grade 9, Thunder Bay

"How nice that the board has found extra cash to build a brand new school while stuffing inner-city... kids like sardines into 'repurposed' spaces."
Patty Hajdu, Thunder Bay.

"It's your money, people dutifully submitted as taxes. Dig in your heels, do what you have to do to send the message to those in power."
Sybil Debrusk, Thunder Bay

"I hope the district municipal league committee that was formed hasn't given up on the possibility of separation just because Southern Ontario threw us a few tidbits."
Bill Costello, Atikokan, Ontario

"The people of Thunder Bay and the Northwest have heard it all before and watched mills close a month later. There doesn't seem to be much confidence in the system here. Despite industry and community leaders telling us that this is good – people seem less inclined to believe it. It's like the government that cried wolf to them."
Editorial-The Source, Thunder Bay, Ontario

"You just can't paint the whole province with same brush."
Roy Hoffman, Pickle Lake, Ontario

"I live in Northwestern Ontario which has lost more than 6,000 jobs in the last year and a half. Moving to Alberta is cold comfort when you have worked 20 years to build home equity for retirement, but now the home can't be sold."
Bev Sarafin, Geraldton, Ontario.

"It is time to discontinue paying any bills received from Ontario Hydro. They can't cut us all off."
Pearl Lemay, Manitouwadge, Ontario

"Again the province ends in Toronto, and once again our local politicians are grateful for table scraps"
The Source Thunder Bay's community newspaper.

"We lost half of our federal compliment of civil service jobs since (the early 1990's). For the federal government to look at removing even more is very troubling."
Tony Martin, Sault Ste Marie, Ontario

"The government isn't coming to the rescue; we don't have enough voting constituents."
C.B. Thomson, Thunder Bay

"The Ministry of Natural Resources has announced plans to demolish the dam on Onion Lake. The only problem with this plan is that it stinks."
Charlie Kivi, Thunder Bay

"Once again, a McGuinty Liberal government's decision made in Southern Ontario does not take into account the economic reality of the North.
Andrew Foulds, Thunder Bay

And so the Bears cry and whine, their pleading voices falling on the deaf ears of listless politicians in Bear Country. Common Bears in the bush ask, "Is there not one Smoky the Bear politician who can stand up on his or her hind legs and shout: **"FIRE! FIRE THE DAMN RACCOONS!"**

Bear politicians never get to come down from their trees

SILENT VOICES: REGIONAL COMMUNICATIONS & BEAR COUNTRY ARTISTS

"Beebee really likes this piece"
"Yeah, that's because there is food in it."

In many countries artists with vision often lead the way in initiating political change. However, in the N/NW, they are mostly bears in hibernation. Its like when is Rodney Bruin going to write a song about bears and the southern raccoons. When is a playwright going to write a humorous treatise on a raccoon falling off a train in Armstrong, Ontarario? Are all the artists, writers, playwrights, film makers, cartoonists, just colonists in their own turf too? Well, pretty much. None of them seem to be able to write a letter to the editor about their plight.

For such a huge, beautiful area so rich in resources, with a history of Euro-Canadian settlement older than southern Tarana we have in the N/NW no book publishing company, no film production house, no regional magazine, not even a literary quarterly at Lakehead University. So, despite the amazing talent existing between the Sault and Kenora and Thunder Bay and Sandy Lake, the opportunities for communicating to our citizens and the rest of Canada are straight-jacketed. And one thing is for certain, we cannot expect the raccoons to ever give us a fair share of cash from the Ontario Arts Council because they have 10 million energy eating gluttons down there. They need every cent of the limited OAC budget. People in our public art galleries work for love and get stale peanuts for their families. Writers can't obtain any prominence for their works in big box candle stores like Chumpsters. Musicians in the north don't have a decent recording studio to utilize.

The cultural disregard for the N/NW is demonstrated by the rotting away of the Wendell Beckwith site in the forest at Whitewater Lake. For raccoons like MPP Tony Bong from Markham and MPP Peter Corncob from Niagara Centre, Wendell Beckwith might as well be some fictional character from Saturn. The architectural creativity implemented by Beckwith in the design of his log buildings and built by the Slipperjack lads was a unique creation in the middle of the bush. His furniture designs were marvelous as well. To make a long story short Beckwith passed away in 1980 and eventually MNR-the fabled ministry of no results has ended up with the property under the jurisdiction of Wabikimi Park. A plan for the site will take two years it is reported. Of course, by late 2007 there will be nothing left at the Beckwith Whitewater site but sawdust and moss. The point is, that if this unique set of buildings had been anywhere within 500 miles of Tarana it would have be heralded and promoted and MNR would have received the budget to maintain it. Not in the Northwest, no way José!

Cultural institutions in the north are so under funded that, for just one example, the Thunder Bay Historical Society Museum has seven years of donations that have not been cataloged because there is no summer grant money any longer to hire students to do the work. If it was not for volunteers at all our museums in the N/NW there would be little to display to celebrate our exciting past. Not only has our heritage been shredded but our voices have been muffled. The Raccoons have given us a never ending case of laryngitis.

CBQ radio communications in Bear Country have been the victims of an insidious plot. There is not another way to describe the plight of regional radio programming in black bruin land. Whether you recognize this or not bear folks, their plight is your problem. Bears have had their voices silenced by Raccoons in Ottawa. Do you recall when CBQ the regional station in Bear Land had a two hour radio noon program. Bears and Bearettes and

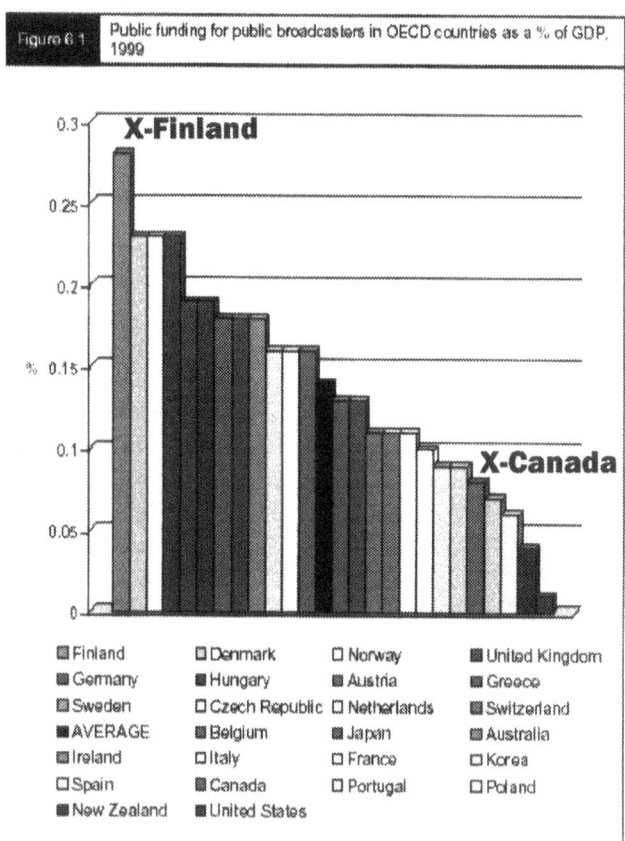

Figure 6.1 Public funding for public broadcasters in OECD countries as a % of GDP, 1999

- ▣ Finland
- ▣ Germany
- ▣ Sweden
- ▪ AVERAGE
- ▣ Ireland
- ▢ Spain
- ▪ New Zealand
- ▢ Denmark
- ▪ Hungary
- ▢ Czech Republic
- ▪ Belgium
- ▢ Italy
- ▪ Canada
- ▪ United States
- ▢ Norway
- ▪ Austria
- ▢ Netherlands
- ▪ Japan
- ▢ France
- ▢ Portugal
- ▪ United Kingdom
- ▪ Greece
- ▪ Switzerland
- ▣ Australia
- ▢ Korea
- ▢ Poland

Bear cubs around the vast north had a way of listening to each others concerns, reminiscences and jokes. When this program was wasted it represented, in one month, the vanishing of 40 hours of political and cultural information for knowing what is going on in Bear back yards. In the course of a year 500 hours of radio voice time disappeared in northern turf. The reasoning from the Baloney and Crouton governments at the time was financial, but the more important political impact was, politicians from afar do not want us to know what the hell is going on in our own forests. The overall Ottawa investment in CBC public broadcasting looks like this. Rankings are expressed as a percentage of GDP.

Finland ranks first of twenty-five OECD countries by spending .28% of GDP on public broadcasting, whereas Canada ranks 22 of 25 countries spending about .07% on public broadcasting in the second largest country in the world. In Bear Country it means our voices are purposely silenced. Mayor Linnforpetesakes is lucky if she can get on CBQ once every two months for two minutes at a time. CBQ's latest fear is that with declining listener rates they may have the station amalgamated with Sudbury which is just down the road-ho ho ho! What has happened to CBQ radio programming is scandalous. The station has no air time for radio documentaries or Northwest forums on the issues of the times. Bear listeners have remained mute at this evaporation of democracy. Its shameful how disengaged we are.

It seems only newspapers in Bear Country have the ability to fight back in documenting the ongoing dismay in nowhere Ontarario. The Dryden Observor, Fort Frances Times, Kapuskasing Northern Times, Kenora Daily & Miner News, Northern Ontario Business, The Thunder Bay Chronicle-Journal, The Source and others are brazenly reporting the voices of their readers. And why not, what have newspaper owners to gain in declining readership and advertising revenues.

When it comes to northern culture the ultimate state of bruin decline over the years is illustrated by the fact that the unenlightened want to throw our curling bears out of the Canadian Briar and to this notion there is little protest. When, indeed, will some Bears take the corks out of their mouths?

COLONIAL MINDS

In the lovely land of the Black Bears all the bears in their dens await the arrival of the King or Queen Black Bear and a court of able supporters to save them from the overbearing black masked lone ranger-looking Rocky Raccoons. How can they be prevented from stealing more wealth from Bear Land? The cries coming from Bear dens all over the northern forests are deafening. Bears don't want to move to the city. They don't want to all go to Fort McMurray change their coats and become Polar Bears. Where, the Bears and Bearettes shout are our leaders? Who will lead us away from the nasty Raccoons? Do any Bear politicians out there have any balls?

"Algoma readily furnishes abundant and interesting themes for the ablest statesmen and the most eloquent orator, and it is high time the hardy settlers selected their man into whose hands they propose committing the interests of such a valuable trust"
(The Weekly Herald & Lake Superior Mining Journal-Prince Arthur's Landing, May 20, 1882.)

How do Bear folk assess the lack of effectiveness of political and corporate leaders in the North/Northwest of Ontario? A wise old Bruin might say

57

that if you have studied your problem closely enough you will have realized that you are a part of it. So, where do all these hardworking Bear- dedicated in most cases- politickers arrive at futile band-aid or zero results for all their effort? There is no representation worth noting in Tarana and Ottawa, but is there no way to surmount the obstacles of being in the invisible middle of Canada where the weather summaries on CBC and CTV regularly jump from Tarana to Winnipeg as if Sault Ste Marie and all the communities in between do not even exist.

The problem many ordinary working Bears say is they have a mentally blinded bunch of leaders that actually have reverence for the centres of power in Tarana and Ottawa. They appear to hustle at times but they are fixated. They are wired lackeys to an imperial power held by the Tarana legislature. The N/NW is in its totality a Golden Horseshoe colony. There is no denying this.

When you live as a colonist you know it. The dictionary describes a colony as, "a group of people remaining subject to a parental state; a body of settlers or their descendants." The Bear residents in the north are, in their 21st Century day to day lives, colonists. Being a colonist is a juvenile condition and being a bear politician in a Raccoon legislature is a juvenile existence. The political immaturity of all kinds of elected Bears in the N/NW boggles the brain.

What happens when Bear people send their political leaders to Tarana? How do they get so, well, dumb? Is it Tarana water they are drinking or the food in the parliamentary cafeteria? One thing the GTA Raccoons teach our northern politicians is the 'Raccoon Shuffle'. It goes like this: three steps forward, two big steps backward, then side step, side step, turn around and take another step back. The idea is they will be seen as moving all the time.

The fact is with northern political Bears like this, ordinary Bear folks are just plain humiliated. Too many of the Bears politicians are long in the tongue and short in the gut. Northern Bears are without meaningful representation in a democratic country. Lording over northern Bear folk are their own northern leaders. Colonial MPP's and MP's give a spin on every misguided policy laid on bare heads. Then there are the Imperial Crown Agents, the various elected councils and school boreds who create the false image that they function on community directive, but in reality are just dancing to distant Raccoon set budgets and directives. Next, there are all the Crown Servants in various Ministries who are employees of the imperial knuckleheads in the southeast. All this allegiance and loyalty to centres of authority that have disenfranchised Bears is just not effective and certainly not very smart. There have been in the past tea parties about this situation. Bear people have taxation without representation so many are ready to put the kettle on and pull out the tea bags.

Can Schmoozi, Rowdyson, Aircan and Moroless, Botchup and all the rest of the northern politicians hear the crying Bears and resolve their problems? Not so far.

When northerners elect their whopping number of MPP's and MP's to send off to Tarana or Ottawa this is the singular and narrow extent of their impact as citizens. Because Bears are dealing with parliamentary systems of government their elected reps are drafted into a political party team. The team rules not the needs of the representative's constituency. This team custom individual conflict has been built into the parliamentary system since the beginning of time. The editor of 'The Official Paper of Algoma' described this conflict in this manner back in 1882.

"there is no harm in taking a look at the way Algoma stands in the house. The member at present, Mr. Lyon is a supporter of Mr. Mowat's Government. In this very extensive District we have but one member for the local house, whom, be he ever so clever a man, is incapable of representing us as we should be."

The problem that the N/NW deals with is not the parliamentary system or political party allegiance. The problem is northern Bruins send their provincial representatives to a meaningless jurisdiction. It is a political system with almost no merit for those 240,000 Bears who live in 75% of the territory. Ontarario is one poorly conceived province. It can not be governed from a centralized power base in Tarana. Do politicians in Paris, France think they could govern realistically in Oslo, Norway? We doubt it. Why then would anybody but a Rocky Raccoon in Tarana think they could govern equitably over Kenora?

Every four years Bears send players to Tarana.

Hockey Hamson and Billy Moroless, forwards, and Mitchell Grovel, defenseman, end up with their political skates on in the same arena. They are called to the 'show' on four year contracts. When they get to the show they find 107 other players there and because they are from the boonies they rarely get ice time. During the games they are forced to walk in the stands, sell popcorn and cheer or boo for the teams. They have no impact on the games that are played. This is what northern citizens deal with when it comes to exercising their democratic rights. Their players don't get ice time. What Bears don't understand is why these players bother with Tarana's 'show'. Why don't they make up their own league? Really, how hard could this be? Get a League Convener and start!

In addition to this, Bear northerners appear to have fixations to political parties as if certain political parties were coded into their DNA. The political mind-set in N/NW Ontario has been entrenched for decades in a Liberal trough. Some Bruins ask the question, does voting Liberal create in a person some kind of higher moral credit with God? In a recent letter to the Chronicle-Journal, Ms Climahill congratulated everyone on returning three N/NW Liberal MP's to Ottawa-the Schmoozi, Kenny Botchup and Noyodell Vallee. Climbahill, a twenty-something at the University of Western Ontario goes on to state how she was raised in a Liberal family. Some thinking Bears have news for Ms Climbahill. An intelligent assessment of political choice facing a voter should not be some numb skulled decision like you are cheering for your favourite hockey team. Get deep Climbahill! Service rendered to community, the democratic issues, the quality of the candidate are considerations. Otherwise voting is akin to a ritual of faith. Perhaps polling stations should all be in churches. Perhaps, at Western Ms Climbahill will keep her interest in political shenanigans for she is exceptional as a twenty-something to have any interest at all in the fate of her country and community. Who knows, maybe, some day she will be elected by voters as a member of the Green Party.

The real point for Bears and Bearettes above Lake Superior is not which party they are voting for, but where they are sending their politicians because these representatives end up in an alien Tarana as if it was some kind of Mecca for faithful colonials.

Far too many old guard Bears rejoice in all the impossible and futile connections with Tarana that they can. It seems that King Raccoon Galton's chief of staff, his Don, Don Guile was actually raised in Thunder Bay. He graduated from Port Arthur Collegiate. You know the one, the handsome old historic building in the core of north side Thunder Bay that the Lakehead Bored is going to close down or trade away. Well, whoop-tee-do about Don Guile. He's a raccoon person now, servant to the southeast. Where was he when McDinty removed Ontario manufacturers (and Thunder Bay Bombardier) from favoured status on provincial production orders on things like rail cars-in Washington? Rumor has it that Raccoon Guile made a trip back to PACI last year and he went to see his old Bear Teacher of Business & Economics. Guile was flabbergasted to see Bear Teacher was using the same tests he had been giving 20 years ago when Guile was a student. "How come you are giving the same tests," Guile asked accusingly. "Ah," Bear Teacher said, "the problematic questions in economics and business are still the same; it's only the politicians economic answers to these questions that are always different."

*

Hail To The Defender of Provincial Rights! In 1893, King Raccoon, Oliver Mowat steamed into Port Arthur and the colonial Bears were happy, so happy for his visit. The Raccoon King was happy too, he ruled. In 2006 King Raccoon Galton McDinty flew into the dilapidated Bear village of Schreiber, Ontario. The colonial Bear Politicians there were so happy, so happy for his three hour visit. The Raccoon King was happy too, he ruled. For over a century now Bear peoples elected politicians have gone down on bended knees to the Raccoon potentates from the southeast.

Young Bears say it is time to start looking to N/NW political and business leaders to unload the raccoons from our political agenda. Take all the illustrious owners of car dealerships in the northwest. These entrepreneurs are hardly able to sell a vehicle to a twenty year old because of the incredible private insurance rates that exist in Ontario. How many more vehicles would they be selling if insurance rates were set by Autopac in Manitoba? A twenty year old in Ontario under his parent's insurance policy on a 1998 Ford Contour pays $2800 a year in insurance. In Manitoba this young driv-

Port Arthur 1893

er would pay approximately $1,150 per year. Don't ever tell the young bear cubs of the Northwest about these differences in vehicle insurance rates because when the plebiscite comes about joining the N/NW to Manitoba or create our own province they are all going to vote for the Manitoba option. Presumably all the car dealership owners are going to vote this way too unless they have a big stake in a private insurance company.

The loyalty and the overriding concern for elected and corporate leaders should be to their communities as well as economic sensibilities. However, when Bear Country sends off MP's and MPP's on their retirement packages its like they have joined inner-city gangs. Liberal MP Mitch Grovel is a fine example, but not the only politician to act like they have had their mouths duck-taped once they get to the governing gang in the east. You can rail all you want in opposition. Once you are in the governance gang you better clap your trap, mister. As long as political riding associations in the North/Northwest maintain the same attitudes to the insults, the ignorance and the general stupidity that comes from the east, there will be no change. We find our politicians using the governing spin on ridiculous decisions or no decisions at all that come from Tarana and Ottawa. Our N/NW political hacks have not demonstrated courage. Grovel, in a same old sermon to the Rotary Club of Thunder Bay in February 2006, commented on the widespread alienation in the N/NW with the Raccoon MPP's. On the idea of a new province within Canada or an adherence with Manitoba, Grovel stated his status quo view. To this Raccoon MPP the concept was not "a particularly good use of energy. We need to get after the provincial and federal governments." Well, gee, Grovel, Bears have been taking this approach for a century. In 2007 when Grovel stands for re-election in a new 107 seat Ontario legislature where the three northern MPP's percentage has dropped to 2% of the urban house he may find himself in the history bin, finding the whole political playing ground has shifted under his stuck in concrete feet.

When MNR and Galton McDinty's Golden Horseshoe crew could not top a $55 million dollar bid by a US Forestry Company for 196,000 hectares of valuable land in the north, Grovel and Moroless and MNR Monster Rocky Rumsey should have crossed the floor and signed in as independents. Could they possibly protest in this assertive fashion? No way. They might have had their phones pulled from their offices and their Ipods taken away. Or worse, get put out in the hallway. The loss of their personal prestige-whoa there!

This gang allegiance over the needs and rights of community by politicians that supposedly are elected to represent them is really, really disappointing and letters to newspaper editors scream the dismay of many, many

Bears in the land.

Corporate and business leaders are little better when it comes to adherence to Tarana's mind-numbing policies, or lack of them, for Bear Country. You own a business in the north that needs some advertising revenue and you get your cupcake by biting your lips- ads for your paper, a contract to build a sidewalk here, a garbage bin there, a new building that has no budget to hire people. The Sovereign imperial powers in Tarana and Ottawa are not stupid when it come to diffusing real dissent in the colony. Buy them off with their own money. Give them a trip to Slovenia or China. You need some dough for your company, you belong to the right political party, they Fednor you with a loan. There are a hundred ways to keep a business owner happy and on the ever optimistic hinge of more is coming-someday. But if you operate in this nowhere land all you are ever going to get, really, are scraps off the big table. Bears say decide whether you are just a dog or a real Bear. There is a difference.

For the big corporate players like forestry, well, they don't bother with band aids and scraps when they have serious financial problems. They just shut it down and pack-off-so very sorry about the community, the labor force and their kids, and all that. Forget the schmucks we're out to make bucks. We believe in global rape. We're off to Brazil or China. We have been in this zone long enough and it has been a good ride for our stockholders. We never had to spend much on replanting trees. We have been able to write down our assets and never spend to update and improve our production. We milked this northern cow dry and we're out of here!

Herein, the Ursus Americanus of the N/NW have a very large problem. Bare forests are a mess. Under the dominance of Rocky and the Raccoons we have had a century plus of paltry replanting, little research on boreal growth and linear crown land forest allotments that look like they were laid out by Martians. The high cost of fibre has a lot do with distances wood needs to be trucked. Everything close to the mills in various towns and cities has been cut. Some bears would say raped. "We would first have to take a full inventory (which has never been done), and we would have to begin to develop secondary forest industries which could operate within the sustainable limits of that inventory," wrote long time Bear people activist Peter Lung. Lung's solution is a step toward wrestling with a huge but long ignored reality for Bears. There are dam few decent trees left to climb.

Until Bear country politicians and business leaders start acting like their continuing subservience to the Lord Raccoons in their castles in the east is no longer acceptable, nothing is going to change in nowhere Ontario, no matter how many conferences or meetings are called by worried do-gooders. It is no use for MP Kenny Botchup to call for building a New North upon the rotted outdated colony that is northern Ontario. If he would just introduce a private members bill to create a new province west of Sault Ste Marie, or a bill of adherence to Manitoba, well, that would put Botchup in the history books, but cause him a hell of a lot of flack from status quo dummies. The Schmoozi is a better bet to act on northern aspirations. The tall and lanky Schmoozi reminds one of an Italian Charles DeGaulle and at seventy-two has a record of taking risks. He could possibly bear-down and do all bears a great service. On the other hand, maybe he, Botchup and Noyodell Vallee would all tell Ottawa and Tarana, enough is enough.

Young, more aggressive Bears have seen enough boot licking. In this new century, it is time to change the political playing field in the North/Northwest. It is time for Bears take ownership of their own turf. Canada is a democracy. People have a right to real political representation for their communities. It is time to create meaningful governance in the Canadian Confederation. Leave Tarana and the Golden Horseshoe with their immense problems to solve. Their hands are too full to have any concern for the N/NW. Ninety-nine percent of those people can not tell the difference between a birch and a poplar tree anyway and are of no use to Black Bruins.

Whether one is a politician of whatever stripe, an educator, a corporate person, a carpenter there is one important phrase to deliver to the Raccoons.

No way-No longer!

It is time for Mayor Linnforpetesakes and Mickey Powerless to start taking more trips to Winnipeg than they do to the southeast. It is time for the Chambers of Commerce folks in the N/NW to hold a meeting in Brandon, Manitoba and state the bare facts. What would the N/NW bring to Manitoba, Ah not much, six gold mines, two developing diamond mines, a palladium mine, a phosphate open pit mine, hydro electric potential, a world class DNA lab, cottage country, and so forth.

The time has come for Bears to forget the word, HUMBLE.

THE MINISTRY OF NO RESULTS

I'm telling you Gordie Eel, if a CO shows up I don't needa fishing license but you sure as hell do.

One Bearette asks a spunky First Nations Bearette what she had done in the previous college holiday. She replied, "Oh, I worked for MNR in the Fort (Fort Frances) this summer." What did you do there?" "Oh not much," she said smiling. "it's called the Must Not Rush ministry, you know." "That's a new one on me," the second Bearette replied, "I thought it was called the Ministry of No Results."

All kidding aside in this bare facts story, the Ministry of Natural Resources is the pseudo- government of North/Northwest Ontario. When you ask a person in the north who they work for and they reply, "THE Ministry", you know they are not talking about the Ministry of Health or MTO. This powerful Ministry ruled from Tarana holds an iron fist over 85 to 90% of the land mass in the north. MNR provides large employment and is both a curse and a blessing for northerners. MNR controls forestry, fishing, logging, trapping, water diversion, tourism, and hunting. They own all the black bears too. And the rule is that it is illegal to shoot brother bear out of season unless he is in your kitchen eating steak out of your refrigerator. When you shoot it and drop 400 lbs of gore and blood on your nice tiled floor, then you now own the bear. It's your problem to dispose of it. How is that for a made in Tarana policy? I guess you could say that MNR does not bury their dead. It must be said that since Premier Mike Harrassment was in power all the MNR burial staff were laid off and nothing has changed with Galton McDinty's Raccoon gang.

What is really important is that MNR does own all the land in the north. Period. It is not the people that live here that communally own the land, it is MNR land and their regulations are established in the Golden Horseshoe. If Mom and Pop want to get a chunk of land for a business on MNR turf, they have to have a business plan, maybe apply for a grant and await the result before you proceed or the grant will not apply, once the grant is approved and the plan done it has to be assessed, it has to be revised, it may need a complete environmental assessment, this has to be studied, oh and, by the way, we forgot to tell you that it is necessary to incorporate to get a half hectare. By this point, the project is four to five years old and if the proponent has not passed away by then, MNR will have to say no, you can't get the land, sorry. Your project does not meet our requirements after seventeen meetings with you in the last five years. Really, it is this bad when you want title to a piece of Crown Land, whups, we mean MNR land. For the Raccoons, MNR jealously guards every square inch of Bear turf in the north.

There are a lot of great people in MNR, they are Bear northerners too. They know a lot of their regulations are asinine. Take the case of the little old lady that needed some cash so she decided to sell her deceased husbands dried-up moose horns that were stored in her garage. She put an ad in the paper. For sale: Moose Horns $25.00. A Conservation Officer turns up, buys them, then charges her for trafficking in moose horns. You have to realize if you are a southerner, that while MNR does not own dead bears, they do own dead moose horns that are for sale. Granny goes in front of a judge and argues her case. But you know judges, sometimes the law applies and sometimes it doesn't. With MNR, it always applies. She gets fined $10.00 and the CO does MNR $10,000.00 worth of poor public relations. Go figure!

Bears will always say there are many solid northerners in MNR but they have to play the colonial game if they want to survive in their jobs. Their subservience to Tarana was amplified years ago with the results of the Nipigon-McTree case. McTree, a forestry tech, for some strange reason thought he lived in a democratic province. He leaked a forestry document that involved the rape of the Black Bay Peninsula on Lake Superior to his local NDP MPP Jack Stokes. Stokes raised the forestry issue in the Raccoon people's legislature. All hell broke loose for McTree. He was investigated, castigated, ostracized, suspended, appealed and delayed and, after at least three to four hunting seasons finally got his job back. It was a lesson for all MNR employees who would dare to cross imperial power in far-off Tarana. Keep your trap shut and play the game-Tarana Rules!

Another issue that irks some Bears and Bearettes are Moose tag allocations. A hunter from Manitouwadge finds that he is competing for a tag with hunters from Raccoon Ontario. The northerner's point of view is: "I live in the north year round not just for a month of the hunting season. I pay the high gas prices and heating bills and drive five miles for my groceries. I risk my life on the shitty roads. I give blood to the mosquitoes and black flies during the week we call summer up here and I have to compete for a moose tag with guys from Scarberia."

Speaking of Scarberia, two Raccoon Scarberians get lucky and get moose tags. They go hunting outside of Timmins and are wandering around in the forest with their orange and yellow reflective jackets so they won't get shot by other hunters from London, Ontario. Suddenly and without warning one of the Scarberians collapses and falls to the ground. His partner can't arouse him. It seems he is not breathing. In a panic he calls 911 on his cell phone. He shouts in his phone, "I need help my buddy has collapsed out here in the bush and I think he is dead." The operator replies calmly. "What is your name, sir?" "My name is Tom." "Where are you located Tom." "I don't know somewhere outside of Timmins." "Tom, we can help you. I want you to follow my instructions carefully. Make sure your buddy is actually dead." The operator waits. She hears a gunshot. The hunter comes back on the cell, "Yeah, he's dead."

As far as the North/Northwest is concerned MNR office allocations are wackily skewed administratively. Many of the N/NW regional offices are understaffed. When you look at MNR's organizational chart under MNR Monster Rocky Rumsey, you will find that MNR is divided into three regions, Northwest, Northeast and Southern. About 80 % of the Northeast region (Regional Office in South Porcupine) is in the Bear North/Northwest. Anyway, south of Sault Ste Marie which represents approximately 25% of Ontario's land mass where much land is privately held, there are 22 MNR offices of various kinds. From Sault Ste Marie north to Hudsons Bay and west to the Manitoba border this area representing 75% of the land mass there are 21 offices. How this figures in job distribution across the province Bears can't say with any certainty, only that it looks very much like MNR is significantly underrepresented in the North/Northwest in terms of employment.

Speaking of jobs in the N/NW, 'THE Ministry' is not an easy place to find one. They are so under-funded it is reported the Conservation Officers have to stay in their cubicles because regional offices can't afford gas for their trucks, therefore they can not afford to rent a helicopter either, to go out and check the black bears. They are guessing there might be 100,000 of their hairy citizens out there. Maybe there are even more bears on the boreal forest food chain than they think which brings another story.

A Bear hunter goes moose hunting this past fall with his bull license. He is having rotten luck. All he is seeing are cows, most disappointing. After he sees 8 cows, it occurs to him not one of these gallant creatures has a calf with her. "Where are all the calves?" he asks an MNR biologist. The answer is that nobody knows, but brother bear is high on the list of suspects. The Kenora MNR reports they have dam few moose left. Well, so what, all the Winnie-the-Poo MPP fans from the golden horseshoe could care less. And how much revenue does moose hunting generate yearly-a measly $100,000,000.00 or so.

Our northern MPP Hockey Hampson's words, "MNR has been flat-lined" are lost in the smog of southern Ontarario. Fish culture and fish stocking of speckled trout, lake trout, splake and rainbows are in decline. Yet, John Complainer the President of Northwestern Ontario's Sportsmen Army reports MNR Tarana is spending nearly 5 million bucks a year on a "BearWise" program. Not only do northerners have to give up $40 million per year on the cancelled spring bear hunt, but taxpayers are spending another $5 million on a program that advises people in nowhere Ontarario how to live with the black bruins. Really, MNR Monster Rocky Rumsey does need to go back to Grade One.

Perhaps, when Black Bruins kiss the Golden Horseshoe good-bye, the remaining MNR employees still left in southern Ontario can have their jurisdiction extended to a true natural resource in the south, nuclear power stations.

TRANSPORTATION-
TERRY FOX'S COURAGE HIGHWAY

Getting around Bear Country is an interesting adventure for all the Bruins in the N/NW. One of the routes was named after a great Hero and a lovable brother to all Bears and Bearettes. He was 'The Fox' of all the foxes that have ever trod the grounds in Canada.

At last report Terry Fox's legacy has raised money for cancer research that is now close to $360,000,000.00. In his honour and for his courageous feat the Trans-Canada Highway from the junction of Highway 17 (Arthur street in Thunder Bay south) to Nipigon, some 100+ kms, has been labeled: The Terry Fox Courage Highway. The fact is that Terry's good foot never touched about 1/3 of this stretch. His run ended just past the Municipality of Shuniah Landfill site. This memorial highway represents a short chang-ing of his effort. Why the Terry Fox Courage Highway did not extend to Marathon, Ontario and end at Hodder Avenue in Thunder Bay rests in a mysterious MTO decision made years ago. The fact is it was on the mar-velous scenic hills, overlooking the grandeur of Lake Superior between Marathon and Nipigon, that must have been the most challenging part of his whole run from the east. Climbing and descending those steep hills with cancer in his lungs was the gutsiest part of his feat. It was here above Lake Superior, on one of the potentially greatest scenic vistas in North America

Baby BB on the KOA Hill Hwy # 17

that Terry Fox's improbable run reached its zenith. The Courage Highway, designated as it is, represents a miserly interpretation of his accomplishment.

Other than a couple of unimpressive signs along the Courage Highway the driver would never in his wildest dream ever be aware this route was in honour of a Canadian Hero. The highway-though it is part of the great Trans-Canada-is a secondary road by almost any northerner's standard. It does not even match the quality of many secondary roads in Raccoon land to the south.

The Terry Fox Courage Highway symbolizes for many Bears in the north, the south's complete inability to recognize the unique potential of North/Northwest Ontario. Sure the highway got labeled; sure an acceptable monument got constructed on the outskirts of Thunder Bay. But the Courage Highway is below mediocrity and represents the ignorance and disdain that imperial political power in a different urban dominated culture holds for northern people.

Many northerners refer to the Courage Highway as a cow path or moose trail. It takes a certain amount of courage just to drive on the twisted large sections of it that are spider-webbed with frost cracks. Sure, the cracks were filled with black licorice that sticks to your tires but not the road. It is congested with truck traffic between Nipigon and Thunder Bay. It lacks passing lanes. In sections the telephone poles and some power poles stand tilted alongside creating a sense of vertigo. You feel like somebody put something in your coffee at your last gas-up. Improvements have been band-aid and always done on the cheap, as MTO in the northwest tries to squeeze every cent out of the meager budget allocations they receive from the dimwitted south.

Most of all, the Terry Fox Courage Highway reveals a complete absence of vision and honour for a Canadian hero. As part of the heavily promoted Lake Superior Circle Tour Route, the highway has absolutely nothing to distinguish it. There are no glorious wild flower gardens. There is a paucity of scenic lay-abouts and rest stops with facilities. There is little access to the shores of Lake Superior. The difference between what the Terry Fox Courage Highway could be and what it actually is symbolizes the irreconcilable gap between Bear people and the southern Raccoons.

But wait, Premier Galton McDinty and Monster of Transportation Sweet Sing have a plan, a $1.8 billion dollar plan for highways, but wait again northerners, most of the money will be spent Sudbury and south. It seems MTO wants big traveling numbers on the Courage Highway before any real cash can be committed, but who the hell wants to drive on this highway unless they have to?

It is not just the Terry Fox Courage Highway that is sub standard in the N/NW. Highway 17 from Sault Ste Marie north to White River has an absence of potentially great scenic lookouts. Some of the rock cuts along the highway are so narrow they would not pass a mining inspection for potential rock-fall. (It is from these cliffs that big hairy munsters jump down on your car.)

Highway # 11 from Kirkland Lake to Nipigon is another secondary road through the north. It has much truck travel going west and east with few passing lanes. The highway is mostly level until south of Geraldton to Nipigon. Between Hearst and Longlac, the driver can go for miles without passing and when you drive this route you get the impression your vehicle is about two feet too wide for the road. God knows what the truckers think about this narrow gauge route, especially in the winter when there seem to be a lot of collisions. So, enough about good highways in the northwest, there aren't any.

No wonder tourism promoters in the northwest find it difficult to get Yankees to come across the borders into Bear country. As a Yankee once said, "You Canadians advertise your potholes in the roads, we fix ours."

The missing MTO road sign found in the ditch on the Trans-Canada Highway between the Sault and Wawa.

NORTHERN TOURISM

How can we get the black bears off our substandard northern highways that have the greatest Moose-on-the-Loose signs anywhere in the western world? Okay, We're teasing about the bruins. They don't really like that hot tarmac under their feet. The moose, however, do symbolize the paucity of tourist attractions in the north. If you drive from Barrie in southern Ontario and take Highway # 11 north through Cochrane to go to Thunder Bay you have a 100% chance of seeing a Tyrannosaurus Rex and a Flying Saucer and 1% chance of seeing a moose. You can drive from the Manitoba border to Sault Ste Marie and see a hundred moose signs, but the kids keep shouting, "When are we going to see a real Bullwinkle, Mom?"

Here in the north we have a gallant ungainly looking resource that a tourist cannot see anywhere unless they happen to be very lucky. Sure, there is a castrated Moose monument in Dryden, Ontario that is not the real thing. (Just how politically correct can you be?) The fact is, that you have a better chance to see a Llama or a Buffalo on the drive from Kenora to the Sault than a moose. So, why is there not somewhere in the N/NW an experimental moose station that tourists could go and see real moose. The absence of such an attraction is just one example of how little financial effort, creativity and implementation is made in the tourism sector. Bears know that one of the barriers to any such attraction is the rigor mortis in MNR Tarana.

Bullwinkle and his pal the pussy cat in Longlac, Ontario (photo by Russ Evans)

They own all the moose until you shoot one with a license. Or if you hit one with your SUV despite all the yellow and black signs, and if you are still living then you can own that dead moose for your trouble. The point is that with this MNR pseudo government holding so many facets of N/NW resources in their portfolio the only way a moose attraction is going to occur is if they approve and implement it. Don't hold your breath. And one could say the same thing exists for wolves, caribou, fish and tourists getting a good look at every other critter in the north.

In the 19th century tourist activities on Lake Superior were many. These activities were extensive and fostered by the fact there were no substandard roads to ride. Believe it or not, people took weekend boat cruises to Duluth and Duluth people came to the Lakehead. People were not wusses in those days. Families went on day cruises to Isle Royale and Silver Islet. In the past, there were hardly any fatalities on Lake Superior involving passenger boats. To-day we have radar, sonar, vhf marine radios, global positioning systems and an excellent Coast Guard reporting marine weather updates three times in a 24 hour period. We also have faster and sturdier vessels.

So can a retired couple from Minneapolis drive to Thunder Bay, take a nicely designed 90' modern passenger boat and cruise to Silver Islet for tea, then proceed east between the beautifully sculpted islands and lighthouses of the north Ontario shore, go up Nipigon Bay and overnight at the Red Rock Inn, then proceed on to Rossport for another overnight stop and return to the Lakehead by a different route? Of course the answer to this is no. It's a resource untapped and the N/NW if full of untapped tourist opportunities.

At the end of the summer season in 2005 the small cruise boat that stayed within the confines of the Thunder Bay Port went out of business. Tourists have stopped coming over the Pigeon River Border in droves and locals just never utilized enough of this summer service. Perhaps the attraction was not deep enough and too restricted in the confines of the harbor to draw a clientele. The two largest attractions around Thunder Bay are Old Fort William and Kakabeka Falls. When it comes to waterfalls in the region a tourist could spend two days seeing some interesting waterfalls, if people only knew where they are. When it comes to creating and marketing tourist locations that Bruins have in the forests, it must be admitted they have a failing report card.

The record as it stands is we can not expect investment from the imperi-

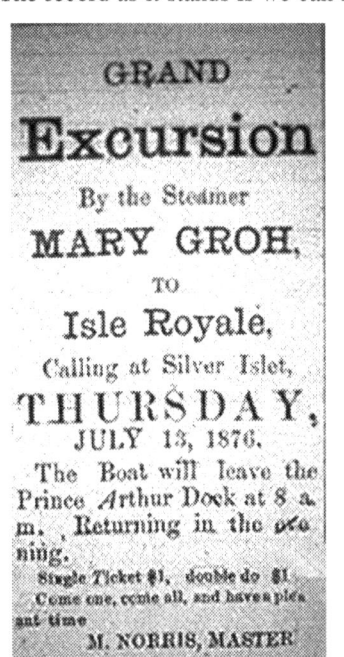

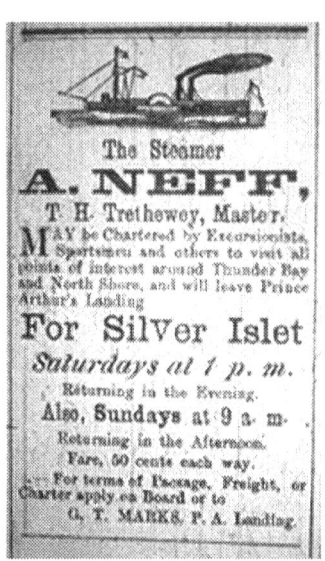

al south for developing tourism opportunities in the N/NW. The last significant capital investment in the north was in the previous century in the construction of Old Fort William and that's it.

In terms of winter tourism there were once six ski operations in the Thunder Bay hills now there are two struggling along. Will there ever be a Nordic Ski Jumping Championship in Thunder Bay again? Not likely the federal government and the province have written us off and frankly we have all let them get away with downsizing after downsizing. Our local politicians are not going to stand up for the north unless they know in certain terms that they will have one session careers if they get no results.

For as long as any one can remember, the solution to tourism problems in the north are seen as a marketing problem. If only we had the right marketing tools, an effective marketing campaign, for our potential visitors in Europe or the United States then everything would improve. Wrong thinking! For example, just this week TB Source (Lindsay La Fraugh) wrote in an article that the six Northern Ontario Regional Tourism Associations-Algoma Country-James Bay Frontier-North of Superior-Ontario's Near North-Rainbow Country and Sunset Country "are looking for ways to work together to enhance the tourism industry." Web sites, fancy magazines and brochures do not cut it. It is what is not in these informational documents that is the essential point. What we do not have in the N/NW is enough tourist infrastructure. New attractions with tourist retention time are desperately needed before you can get visitors to come. Some attractions need add-ons and enhancement. It is easy for the Raccoons to spend a few bucks every year to subsidize tourist associations. What the north needs is many more attractions. For example can a Raccoon and his litter drive to the Sault, get on a train go along Lake Superior to Thunder Bay? Is there a marine museum in Terrace Bay yet? Does the train stop in Rossport for lunch? Is there a hockey school in the summer in Cochrane? Until meaningful money goes into tourism infrastructure the north will not get the tourists except for the hunting and fishing folks.

So what is northern tourism to those snail crunching, egg stealing, long tailed city Raccoons? Lip service only. In corn country though, tourism is a $300 million loan to a plugged-into-the-cabinet guy, David Showman, for the Tarana production of Lord of The Rings. Even some Raccoons shouted foul about this McDinty gift. "At a time when Ontario has a $1.6 Billion deficit (McDinty) spends millions on singing hobbits?" (No wonder these southerners could not afford to buy Abitibi land in the North.) The only-northwesterners that will be seeing the singing, prancing hobbits will be the

Bears three so-called political reps in Tarana.

To change this bizarre approach from the imperial southeast people have to start using their ballots for progressive developmental change. Bruins will have to learn there is a difference between politics and religion and between politics and ethnicity.

Unless we detach ourselves from our long soured relationship with the MPP's in the Golden Horseshoe we will always live in a colony and our families destinies will continue to be in the often belligerent hands of a distant political power.

Waterfalls Moraine Lake Creek, Thunder Bay District

EDUCATION NORTHWEST STYLE

It is well known that for decades the province of Ontarario has spent less money per capita on education than most of the other provinces in Canada. Since the mid-seventies the investment in educational resources has been stop-gap and meager. When Confederation College Pres Pat Ling got a scrap from Galton's gang ($2.1 million with strings on how it can be spent) she was heard to comment, "What you're trying to repair is over 10 years of chronic under funding in post secondary education." For the N/NW where the culture, climate and geography are different factors, formulas for funding devised in the east are so out of touch with northern realities it makes you want to cry or laugh with the bizarreness of southern government policy.

[Question to Premier Galton McDinty on April 12, 2005]

"Before the election Mr. Kennedy [Liberal Monster of Education] said 'Schools are the hubs of northern communities but the Harris-Eves government has failed to support them. We will protect northern schools.'" – Premier – your government is closing their schools –'

[McDinty] –we're not saying that no schools at any time will close ever again in the province of Ontario. What we have said is, we'll change the funding formula so it speaks to the better interests of our students –'

Well excuse the Bears, King Galton Raccoon, we thought they were OUR students.

Unfortunately for the people of Thunder Bay the colonial Lakehead District School Bored, sycophants to King Raccoon in their subservience to southern directives, have forged ahead with school closures. Give them blinders and a task and do they go to work. The energy expelled by Lakehead Bored is admirable but what about the mind-set of this totally city living group of seven citizens. Following the previous educational policies of Premier golfer Mike Harrassment, this Bored initiated a twenty-year study on the needs of their students. Right off the top, twenty years is a ridiculously long time for any study. We could all die from bird flu twice by then. Even the Soviets in the Communist era in Russia only had the nerve to do Five Year Plans. The second factor in this group of southern Ontario loyalists is that they hired a Tarana firm, C.N Watson & Associates from Mississogi. What an error. Some economists from Helsinki or Oslo might have been more in touch with our northern culture. What is so disheartening about this Bored is that they have unwittingly behaved like feudal tacksmen of old that took it as their sacred duty to clear the highlands for their imperial chieftains. In this case, it is a clearing of the countryside around Thunder Bay and the downtown core of Thunder Bay North.

The final report of the Watson study was shocking. Using phony spin words like enhancement, school consolidation, right-sized, financially sound, opportunities, centres of excellence, attendance boundaries and all of this based on a funding model concocted on the orders of the urban raccoons from the Golden Horseshoe.

When the final report of Watson and associates descended the results were: Nineteen (19) schools were slated for closure starting in 2005. One might have thought that of seven Bored members that somebody would have resigned, deciding not to accept the alien formula imposed upon them. No bloody way that these colonial mind-set characters would have the courage to reject the raccoons. Nope, they have executed the Tarana plan against all the vociferous protest. The Lakehead Bored is writing themselves into Bear Country history as the most subservient group of upside down colonial agents to ever disgrace themselves in the North/Northwest.

It also must be said there is a lot of talent in the members of the Lakehead Bored, but it would seem they have no sense of themselves in a historical context, a political context and a community context. They delude themselves with the appeal of $70,000,000.00 worth of mega projects like a new $30 Million dollar high school to be built on a golf course adjacent to Lakehead University. Port Arthur Collegiate and Hillcrest High School on the north side of the city are to be closed. Yikes! Doesn't this give Heart of The Harbour businessmen a coronary? Well, no thought was given to the fact their decision would result in emptying the north side core even more. One also has to ask, is there no realization from either the Lakehead Bored or the University what the implications might be to have 15 and 16 year old gals that look 21 sideling through the dorms at the University looking to have a beer and other pleasures? This is nuts. Many university students have complained the construction of such a high school is going to alter the existing pleasant ecology of the LU campus. Surely an environmental assessment is in order. The Regional Hospital is only blocks away from this site and the thought of roads packed with school buses coming and going about the entrances to the hospital really make one wonder about this location for a high school. To add to the congestion in this area is a Flying J Truck Stop a block away and Panda Developments planning to build a 96 unit nearby. This is progressive? For this new 'enhanced' high school on LU grounds a change of zoning will have to be approved by the Thunder Bay Council. Surely the Council will put their foot down on this out of-their-minds Bored of Education and save them from disaster. (Fortunately the Thunder Bay Council did just that.)

A round of talks with citizens about the aforementioned massive closures has "left parents angry and frustrated that the board isn't seriously considering their input." The Bored is, however, very seriously considering the imperial directives from the Raccoons from the tarmac lands in the east. With recent shutdowns in 2005-06 which will result in a startling change of demographics, some Bruins wonder if a new high school will ever be relevant.

It should be noted that school boreds in Ontarario can not establish their own funding needs. Premier Harrassment of yesteryear determined all funding for public education would be decided by MPP raccoons and their administrative civil servants in Tarana. So school Boreds, especially those in the north dance to a very distant tune. In the case of the Lakehead Bored are they ever in step with their colonial masters. Perhaps many of them hope to go to Tarana eventually as MPP's, become mute and collect fat pensions.

The impact of frugal education policies in Ontario create some quite strange behaviour and not just with the Lakehead Bored. Take Lakehead

University's latest 2005 gambit-opening a campus where? Not in Kenora, but on southern Ontario turf at Orillia. Is this the mandate of a north Ontario university, to open a campus some 1000 southern kms away? "This gives us opportunities to grow and develop in new ways," LU President Freddy the Eagle was quoted as saying to Kathryn Lyzun in The Source. Well, no kidding. LU is hoping to have between 100 and 200 hundred students on the Orillia campus in September of 2006. The question raised here is what is really going on. How come these 200 or so students just can't come directly to the LU campus in Thunder Bay? Supposedly LU is in the same province as Orillia. Are students down there afraid of the bears? How is this southern expansion being funded? Freddy the Eagle is hoping that Orillia students will come north and maybe some will pass through as they head for BC and Alberta for jobs. One expects the return to the northern campus will be minimal. It all seems so strange. Maybe the sport teams from Orillia will adopt the name Thunder Raccoons as apposed to Thunder Wolves since the wolves were all wiped out in the urban south a century ago.

Elsewhere, the community colleges in the north at Sault Ste Marie, Thunder Bay, and Timmins plug away with astonishing gaps in their funding. Funding again based on a made-in Tarana formula. At Confederation in Thunder Bay they have had to lay-off their mail person. The library and info centre has an anemic budget for obtaining supplies. Programs have been cancelled. The Crown servant President of Confederation is salaried at $200,000 plus per year until her retirement by a syrupy board of mostly retread Liberals while instructors in the institution dig in their pockets for supplies. Not a word ever comes out of the Bear Bored members mouths. It's disappointing.

Everything in the north is run on the cheap when it involves funding from the imperial legislature in the south.

Just when are Bears in the colony going to smarten up? Well, the answer to this is easy. As the old Bear elder said, "change comes when there is a cessation of stupidity."

Then, there is the positive of the new northern medical school at the under funded state of the art, Thunder Bay Regional Hospital and its tie in with a Sudbury partner in the south. Don't the Raccoons know it takes 10 hours of speeding on the Trans-Canada cow path to get from Sudbury to Thunder Bay? Don't the Raccoons get the differences in space in the Northwest, the distance from Sudbury to Thunder Bay is about the same as the distance from Warsaw, Poland to Paris, France and the last atlas we consulted has four European countries in between these cities. Ya gotta wonder how this medical school relationship is going to fly. Well, I guess the med students will have to fly if they are going to get from one class to another in the same day. The only reason there is a Medical School in Thunder Bay is that Ernie Evening in his run for leadership of the PC party made a deal with locals; your support for a medical school. So we have a much needed Med School but why is it formally attached to Sudbury, so inefficiency can reign supreme?

A sign in the Lakehead Bored of Education Parking Lot

HEALTH

The Galton Gang of MPP Raccoons in Tarana have now assumed a new set of dictatorial powers in the passing of Bill 36 that will create 14 Local Health Integration Networks (LHINs) for the Province of Ontario. The N/NW Areas LHIN 13 and LHIN 14 are so large that the appointed dicktaters of these northern areas who will be paid about $230,000.00 per year will have to access an F-18 jet fighter so they can get around these two northern health colonies. LHIN 13 and LHIN 14 represent, geographically, more than two thirds of the whole province. The distances are vast.

The Liberal Galton Gang spin on the LHINs is they are constructing a "true health system". What they are actually constructing is an iron clad centralized system of health care controlled by the Health Monster and his cabinet cronies. The bottom line of Bill 36 is a downsizing of Health Care in Ontarario. It will be bad enough for southern Ontario. In the north/northwest it will be worse because of our distances and other northern factors that create higher costs. You can bet your boots LHIN 13 and 14 will be funded on an urban set formula that will create real difficulties for the many people in remote communities in the north.

Just how the LHIN 14 will deal with Tom Closson's Report on the shortcomings of health services in the Northwest is a question yet to be addressed. Closson was appointed by the Tarana MPP raccoons to look for solutions to the various inadequacies in the Thunder Bay area. Closson's report was well done and many of his recommendations (accurate and needed) in terms of acute care in the region, heart surgery and other services at a cost of $112 million. With the LHIN budget being established in Tarana one suspects Closson's recommendations will soon be forgotten as the imperial servants on the LHIN board execute alien directives. Critics of the LHIN plan warn that because many health services will be open to a bidding process one can expect the growth of private suppliers. What happens if the Lake of The Woods Hospital wins a bid for supplying all the hernia operations in the northwest? This means a person from Marathon will have to drive for 8 hours to Kenora to receive treatment. This is a fictitious example but you get the idea of what may happen.

The Nishnawbe Aski Nation leaders in the boreal uplands are worried about the Local Health Integration Networks as well. Deputy Grand Chief Alvine Fiddbar was quoted in Wawatay News, saying: "LHINs reduce local control of health delivery of existing First nations health authorities, makng the system more centralized and culturally insensitive than it already is."

Ontario's Monster of Health Smotherwoman apparently had some of his own amendements to the LHIN act rejected by brother raccoons. The implementation of LHINs 13 and 14 does not bode well for the widely spread Bears in the north country.

The next Galton move in health care is the financing of hospitals through P3s, public- private partnerships. This move has brought a strong retort from the RNAO (Registered Nurses Association Ontario) who claim that financiers who build these hospitals add real costs to the Health budget and reduce public control over health. "The companies make their profit through the financing deals, the long term privatization of some hospital facility management and support services, user fees and service charges for patients and their visitors and private development on hospital grounds." A P3 hospital policy "creates a new and powerful stakeholder group invested in dismantling Medicare." Hospitals up for sale on the Tarana stock market; this is real Raccoon progress in the 21st Century?

MAKWAH PEOPLE
TREATY THREE-TREATY NINE & ROBINSON
SUPERIOR FIRST NATIONS

In the great rich lands of Bear Country the Makwah people have been here longer than anybody else. They know about Ursus Americanus because they relate to Black Bear as another person. There is no 'the' in front of Bear in their ancient language. Makwah people know all about living in a colony ruled by distant and alien Raccoons. This is their important part of this present day story.

As far as is known there has never been a First Nations Aboriginal person from the North/Northwest in the parliaments in Toronto or Ottawa. It is noteworthy that after over a century of elected legislatures in these two southern cities no First Nations person from Makwah Country has ever showed up to speak for their people. Nor will there ever be an Aboriginal parliamentarian from no where in Ontario under the current political jurisdictions- which are designed to make certain this never happens- since the boundaries in the northwest run north-south as opposed to east-west. Thus, First Nation populations on the Hudson Bay coast and the boreal uplands are filled with Euro-Canadian populations south of them. The Raccoons will point out of course that James Bartleman, an Aboriginal from Muskoka is the current Lieutenant-Governor of Ontario. It's too bad he doesn't have a veto on the atomic characters in the Toronto legislature. As nice a feature as it is for we northerners to have good man Bartleman as the current Gov of the Province it doesn't cut any ice when it comes to politics. Treaty communities in the north are pretty much restricted to dealing with Ottawa when it comes to major issues.

The Treaty Nine and Treaty Three organizations in particular have been blessed over the years with some astute leaders. One can only surmise what their take would be on a new province in Canada or an attachment to Manitoba by the North/Northwest. One thing is certain though. Without First Nations support for a change in provincial jurisdiction of the Bear lands there will be little opportunity for other political leaders to alter the current ridiculous situation. Possibly there is common ground.

Native communities in the North/Northwest are all plagued with similar problems to the communities south of them. Their community issues, however, are compounded to the tenth power in terms of employment and economic opportunities, health issues, transportation difficulties, and education. Suicide rates among their cubs are a disgrace to Canada and the scourge of diabetes in some northern towns are the highest on the planet.

For First Nations leaders in these organizations, the present Ontario legislature might as well be on the moon. Will the Beardy from Bearskin Lake and Thunder Bay, the current Chief of Nishinabe-Aski Nation ever be invited to address the Raccoon legislature in regard to the long ignored and forgotten 49 reserves and communities of the north? Not bloody likely. Governor Arnold Schwarzenegger of California has a better chance for an invite to the urban legislature (to put the case for reinstatement of executions in Ontarario) than any Chief from NAN or Treaty Three does.

It is worth noting that a Governor General of Canada has never visited any of the reserves in the Treaty Nine area. Perhaps this is because the representatives of the Queen are more inclined to foreign destinations as with the excursions of the last Gov than to go to the struggling communities in Makwah country. These communities remain out of sight and out of mind for urbanites unless there is a tragedy, like poisoned water or a jail burning down with prisoners locked inside.

In a new democratic alignment in the north many of these issues can be abated by the presence of several First Nation parliamentarians sitting in a forum that gives them additional voice beyond Ottawa. Makwah support for the oncoming divorce is a must if all northerners are going to finally reject their colonial status.

First Nations Communities-a View from the North

89

And believe it First Nations folks know all about the inequities of being colonials in their own country.

Many of the native communities and settlements on the Hudson Bay coast and uplands are no longer tiny. Sandy Lake, Deer Lake and North Spirit Lake kindred communities on the Severn River system have a combined population of about 3,000 people. Pikangikum and Poplar Hill on the Berens River have over 1,500 inhabitants. Fort Severn on the Hudson Bay coast approaches 500 persons. Fort Hope on the Albany has well over 1,000 residents and all of the communities have significant off-reserve members that live in Winnipeg, Thunder Bay and elsewhere.

One hopes First Nation support for a new province or an adherence to the Buffalos in Manitoba will gain strong support because of the additional voice they will receive in their own affairs. If their leaders step forward for a N/NW province in Canada First Nations Bears and Bearettes should be given the honour of naming this newly enfranchised land. After all, these brothers and sisters to all northerners have been here the longest. Maybe they will name our new province, Makwah after you know who, our Black Bears.

ACTS OF REBELLION

For well over a century the N/NW has been the hinterland colony of the populated urban southeast in Ontario. From the days of Simon Dawson to the final usurpation of the northwest in 1912 there have been ineffective stirrings for democratic representation for northern citizens. The last outcry came from, believe it or not, North Bay, Ontario a mere 345 kms from Tarana, a three and a half hour drive. This little hop to Toronto is an indication of just how internally focused the Queens Park legislature is in its urban concerns when citizens from nearby North Bay feel remote from the seats of political power.

The political stirrings from North Bay were led by Ed Deibel. Diebel and the Northern Ontario Heritage Party he founded contained a number of economic concepts for the north that still have much relevance today. (There is reference to them in the next section.) In the course of his perambulations around the north he collected 6,000 signatures on a petition requesting a vote be held on Northern Ontario becoming a separate province. He took the petition to William Wily, the PC Premier of the day.

What a totally wrong move. Taking a petition to your oppressor to ask for release is useless and politically dumb.

Hopefully, in the 21st Century political leaders in the N/NW will not sidle down this one-way street. Municipalities, townships, improvement districts this time will put such a plebiscite to their constituents. If a positive result is obtained a new N/NW Assembly should be appointed by municipal leaders and this Provisional Assembly deals only with Ottawa bypassing the reactive raccoons altogether. (The details of southern Ontario's indemnification to the north for a century and a half of extraction and wanton mismanagement can be worked out later.)

At this writing a small insurrection in the N/NW is underway from the western end of Ontario. Led by Mayor Aircan, supported by Mayor Crass, municipal politicians from Fort Frances and others in the Kenora District Municipal Association, a Canada Public Policy Research Trust will investigate the pros and cons of adherence to the Buffalo people or the establishment of a Bear Province. Municipalities across the north will be asked to join this undertaking and contribute dollars to the undertaking. Since all the facts and figures are pretty much available this research should be completed in months, not years.

One of the questions is, will municipal councils, especially those in Thunder Bay, Hearst, Kapauskasing, Timmins, Greenstone and Sault Ste Marie support this modest step to better democratic representation for their citizens? Debate over this small step at the municipal level will really bring out the levels of colonial mentality fixated in local politicians around the north. Take Mayor Linnforpetesakes, she holds her political cards very close to the chest, but some Bruins surmise her political plotting from the Chair of The Lakehead District School Bored to the Mayor of Thunder Bay is onward to be an MPP in Manitoba and then the Premiership of Manitoba or the new Bear Province. Surely, she would not want to go off to be forgotten as a Martinet for Tarana.

When the rest of the suited and aspiring politicians in Bear Country held their annual Nowhere Ontario Municipal Association meeting in Thunder Bay at the end of April, 2006 some squeaks of discontent were heard. But, you can bet none of these aspirants have husbands or wives crying over the kitchen table over vanished jobs and foiled opportunities. The Nowhere Municipal reps talk of a "Northern Ontario Municipal Act" that would give the right to collect tax dollars and provide tax incentives in Bear Lands. This idea is almost funny. It's hard to imagine Betsy the Bear Princess telling Rocky, "Rocky dear, I want to have my own room but still live in your house."

It is reported the 2,240 jobs recently lost in Thunder Bay is equivalent to 385,000 jobs being lost in Tarana. It is hard to imagine the King Raccoon of Tarana just eating clams and doing nothing if this was actually the obliteration of jobs in his back yard. Among this old guard of spinning politicians at NOMA, the word, "separate" was only spoken in the sanctity of the washrooms.

DIVORCE PROCEEDINGS

Why do divorces cost so much?
Because they are WORTH it.

"I refer to the question of the enlargement of the Province, especially eastward to Lake Superior or Thunder Bay. This question is of utmost importance to the people of Manitoba. It may be said by some, what difference is it to you what province you are in, or through what province your traffic passes? It may be all the difference in the world–. You have heard about this notorious boundary award–What is called an award was found, not professing to have been determined on the merits of the question as regards evidence –Not from a legal point of view, but purely and simply a convenient boundary –we only ask that the question should be fairly and legally determined on its merits. We want the connection with Lake Superior within our province if it can be secured –"
The Honourable C.P. Brown, Minister of Public Works of Manitoba
November, 1882

Just how do we divorce Rocky and those pesky southern Raccoons? Well, Bears might be a tad slow moving on hot days but when the bruins take-off over a 100 yards in any race, a horse or a raccoon is in big trouble. Bear people also know a secret that is only whispered to those in the den. The secret is: the Raccoons want a divorce. It's true. They just can't admit it publicly. Like a disgruntled husband who can't leave his wife so he just abuses her to the point where she walks out. Then he says to his male friends, "the bitch left me." He has been done so wrong! If he had just walked out on her the solid guys would have ridiculed him behind is back. This is the way the Raccoons are treating Bear folks. They want us to leave and understandably so. Galton and his Raccoons have immense problems in the GTA and corn country. We Bears almost feel sorry for him. They have Atomic problems, Electrical problems, Gun problems, Transportation Problems and Financing Problems. So, that's the secret that's being let out of the bag here. The Raccoons want a divorce.

There may be a paltry effort by Raccoon political parties to cozy up to dis-enchanted Bears; however when you have a continual migraine a couple of aspirins are basically useless as a cure to your condition. Bears know this. They will not be swayed by scraps and too-late half-measures.

The thing is Bears will stand up on their back legs and tower over the Raccoons for the first time in centuries. Bruins divorce the corn eaters by having cities, municipalities, improvement districts, and reserves hold plebiscites. NDPer Hockey Hampson and The Schmoozi should be making a few trips to Winnipeg to see if a joint N/NW-Manitoba Committee can be established to investigate the merits of a union. They should ask Garibaldi Doer if they can talk to the Buffalo legislature.

If Bears can only convince the old guard of yesteryear who they have unwittingly put into elected office to serve the interests of Tarana to do this first step. Fortunately, many of our elected officials, municipal, provincial and federal do have IQ's above average so they might even vote yes to test the N/NW people's take on proceeding with the divorce.

Some of our provincial politicians actually do have skills, initiative and drive. They are, after all, complete nobodies down in Golden Horseshoe country. Perhaps Hampson or the chatty Mitch Grovel would like to become the Premier of Manitoba or the first Premier of the Bear Province. After all, what politician can't change his or her mind about anything? There will be those among corporate and political leaders who are so reactive and so attracted to Tarana-like horseflies to raw flesh- Bears will just have to turf them out of office. What about our devoted Political Riding Associations-the backroom people behind our elected politicians? As their constituents scream about the lack of justice in the wilderness the political riding association members in the N/NW are quieter than cemeteries at midnight. Real bears say, quit taking prozac. Get an edge. Tell Tarana to piss-off. Get proactive for the beaten up people in the north.

We send our Liberals, Conservatives, NDPers and Greens to Manitoba for some political chats. Test the waters. Tell them all the positives we could bring to the west, like diamonds, gold, base metals, phosphate, hydro electric power, steel, decent ski hills, some manufacturing, paper mills, cottage country and wind power and a load of talent. It might not be that hard a sell. Remember, half of Manitoba is in Kenora, Ontario in the summertime anyway. They do like us. We even sell them water from Shoal Lake to the City of Winnipeg so they have mix for Kool-Aid on their sweltering summer days.

If that's not a go, all the municipalities and reserves in the N/NW appoint members to a provisional assembly to lay out our new provinces' electoral units. How many seats are we going to have for 246,000 or so people. Eight thousand people to an MPP is sensible so we have a legislature of 30-32 seats. Just think of it northerners-phoning your MPP in the capital city of Geraldton or Terrace Bay or wherever and not getting an answering machine. How lovely!

Ottawa-the Feds are going to have to approve our new status. Bears will have to hire a couple of the legal beagles that saw the set-up of Nunavut. The paperwork must be done. Will Prime Minister Conservative Stevey Haaper support us in our quest for real democratic representation for our communities? Well, maybe. You know he loves those forever Liberal GTA Raccoons. (Some 70% of 1,000 Buffaloes surveyed in Manitoba would agree to merging with the N/NW in a March, 2006 CBC Radio/Canada poll.)

Let's get a move on Mayor Linnforpetesakes, Mayor Aircan, Mayor Rowdyson and Mickey Powerless, order your bumper sticker now. DIVORCE THE RACCOONS! (And vote for us.) Pooed-off Bears are going to get another sticker, "BEARS RULE THE NORTH."

If the Province of Manitoba decides they just could not handle all the wealth we would bring to them, we'll just have to forget this possible marriage and go it alone. Manitoba may not be in the best interests of Bears anyway. Sure Bruins would get 10-15 seats, but Winnipeg, the city state rules Manitoba now.

Perhaps a new Province is in order. It's all doable. Remember little Prince Edward Island became a province in the Canadian Confederation with a tiny island full of potatoes and 87,000 citizens in 1873. Most of their island was owned then by British non-residents, the same situation that exists in the N/NW now with Tarana's MNR owning all the land. If PEI could join Canada as a province nearly 150 years ago with horses and buggies Bears can do it now with snow machines and the internet. March on brave black bears! By the way, PEI nowadays has only 137,000 residents about half the present population in the N/NW.

So let's send a message to Stevey Haaper in Ottawa.

To the Prime Man of All Ministers in Canada,
The Right Honourable Stevey Haaper

Dear Stevey;

We, the Bears of the N/NW appeal to our family relationship with you as a Grizzly from the west of Canada. While we humble Bears of north Ontarario are not so endangered as your relatives are, we hope you can clearly see our sad situation and act on the Bear Manifesto that follows.

P.S. Would you mind, Stevey, sending 10 gallon barrels of Clover Honey (unpasteurized of course) to the Bear Pits in the following places; Kenora, Red Lake, Fort Frances, Dryden, Thunder Bay, Greenstone, Hearst, Kapuskasing, Timmins, Smooth Rock Falls, Wawa, Chapleau and Sault Ste Marie. We never get any sweets from Tarana.

Thank you very much-Bear With It!

THE BEAR MANIFESTO

Whereas the Country of Canada is a democratic domain believing strongly in the principle of just representation for its citizens in a parliamentary system of government, we the great Black Bear peoples of the North/Northwest Territory of Ontarario place this statement in the pursuit of our undeniable democratic rights.

Whereas the Bears of the large Territory of N/NW Ontario are disenfranchised by a minimal and meaningless representation in the distant Raccoon Legislature in the Province of Ontarario;

Whereas the Bears of N/NW Ontarario endure the burden of taxation, arbitrary legislation without meaningful representation in the aforesaid Raccoon Legislature;

Whereas the resources and wealth of Bear Territory have been basely mismanaged and squandered for over a century by the distant Raccoon Legislature of Ontarario;

Whereas the resources and wealth of Bear Territory are usurped and not equitably shared with Bears by the distant Raccoon Legislature;

Whereas the social pursuits and economic future of Bears in the N/NW of Ontarario are held in a culturally inappropriate Raccoon Legislature.

We the disenfranchised Bears of the N/NW Territory in the present Province of Ontarario doth request that Parliamentarians of the Government of Canada give meaningful attention to our sad state of affairs inflicted upon us by an unjust Raccoon governance.

Further, that the Government of Canada initiate, forthwith, the legislation that will allow the loyal Bears of the N/NW Territory to exercise their democratic right to determine their political future within the confines of our young evolving country, Canada.

Official signage along the great Trans Canada Highway (ho-ho!) at Gravel River, Ontario.

THE ECONOMICS OF CHANGE

Bears are handsome. Raccoons yuk.

The economics of the Bear country relationship with Raccoon land remind one about the time BB Bear decided to take a trip to Tarana so he hops a freight train out of the north. When he finally arrives three days later he's really thirsty. He sees a neon sign on a building. The sign says, BAR. "I can s-sure relate to that sign," says BB. So he waddles into the bar, goes up to the counter, slams his paw down and says to the waiter.

"I'll have one o' them K-Kokes."

The waiter was dumbfounded, "that hairy bastard looks like he's 7'8". He looks like he could play for the Raptors," he thought to himself.

The waiter quickly brought BB a big bottle of Koke. Now BB had never had a Koke, but he had seen a sign outside of Timmins one time and it was a big picture of Polar Bears drinking Kokes.

BB guzzles the Koke and it fizzed in his mouth and some bubbles came out his nose. His eyes glazed over in pleasure as he drank the big bottle without taking a breath. This tastes way better than gasoline he thought. When he finished he rubbed his mouth with his paw and said, "Wheeuuu. How much money is it for a K-Koke?"

The waiter sized up BB. He can't be that smart was his assessment. "It's ten dollars for a Koke." BB pawed over a $10.00 bill he had found in a garbage dump. The waiter feeling a little more relaxed now that he was quickly paid his money said, "You know we don't get many bears coming into this bar."

"I'm not surprised," BB said, "when it costs $10.00 for a K-Koke."

Getting ripped off by the Raccoons is illustrated by the ineffectiveness of colonial politicians in the north and demonstrated by the Thunder Bay Charity and Sault Ste Marie Charity Casinos. This is a case where those greedy little raccoons know how to outwit the slow moving black bears. Yes, it's a Charity Casino alright, Northerners get to have a fancy casino and a few jobs that pay modest salaries and the raccoons get our charity. Only 5% of the revenue from these dazzling slot machine pits goes to the cities. The latest quarterly pay-out to Thunder Bay is based on a gross of $12.2 million is $613,000.00. By my humble calculation this leaves a mere $11,647,000.00 left to pay the Casino salaries, pay out prize money and pay for maintenance. How would you like to own this business, Kenny Bucksaw?

What have the illustrious City Councils in Sault and Thunder Bay been able to do about this inequity? The answer is zip. All the small charities in the Thunder Bay District have been short changed big time. Minor hockey teams, church organizations and so on find they can't raise enough bingo cash for their recreational and humanitarian efforts. Then there are the Casino horror stories that never make the press. The used book store guy tells a story about a friend of his. A Polish man who came to the north after the Second World War, never married and worked in the bush all his life and prudently saved $200,000.00 to go along with his old age pension. This retiree started going to the casino for something to do. Inside of six months his 200 grand nest egg was gone. This senior became so despondent he commits suicide. His brother in Poland knowing the frugalness of his Canadian sibling flies from Warsaw to bury him and to collect an inheritance. There is not enough money left in the estate to fly the brother back to Poland. The Polish Society people take up a collection to get the saddened brother home. Well, doesn't this make you shake your head? Believe it, there are many stories worse than this one.

The point is that this is the kind of economics that Thunder Bay and Sault Ste Marie Councils are docilely accepting in dealing with those dratted raccoons. It's another rip-off when it comes to electrical rates. Almost everywhere you turn those sharp-toothed raccoons are eating pieces out of your pants or nipping your nylons. So, if we just do happen to find some so-called politicians in the N/NW who decide to stand for a new north they will need to count the assets of social and financial change. Here are some of them.

1. The first order of business will be to move Halloween to September 30 so the cubs don't have to put snow suits on under their costumes.

2. We collect our own sales tax and set taxes on tobacco & other items. (Revenue +)

3. Northern politicians determine the pay-out from Charity Casino's in the North/Northwest. (Revenue +)

4. We set our own stumpage rates. (Revenue +)

5. Bears have their own Brewers Beer and Liquor stores. (Revenue +)

6. Northerners determine how their own Department of Lands & Forests will operate. (Revenue +)

7. Bears decide what our electrical rates are and we sell our excess to

Minnesota and Southern Ontario. (Revenue +)

8. Bruins establish a Department of Mines and what royalties are paid on mining production. (Revenue +)

9. The north decides what schools need to be closed and what funding priorities are.

10. Northerners decide how and by whom automobile and vehicular insurance is to be established for citizens. (Revenue +)

11. Northerners decide how crown land is to be best utilized not a ministry ruled from another domain.

12. Politicians negotiate with Ottawa for federal revenues. (Revenue +)

13. Bruins decide if they want to be a toxic dump site.

14. Northerners actually nurture, develop and implement our tourist potential. (Revenue +)

15. Bear politicians set our social assistance rates for the afflicted, single moms and the elderly.

16. We determine the priorities and funds our health services receive.

17. We decide how and by who our highways are to be maintained and refurbished.

18. Bear politicians take initiatives on peat resources, remaining hydro possibilities, and wind energy for electrical export. (Revenue +)

Many of the economic concepts found in the defunct Northern Ontario Heritage Party manifesto are still current and worthy of consideration. These were strategies like:

Elimination or reduction of taxes on all new manufacturing that produce products in a finished form.

Establishment of a depletion tax fund on non-renewable resources that would be applied to community adjustment.

Creation of a Ministry of Mines.

Developing and expanding research in forestry, metallurgy, paper making, and northern Agriculture.

We have wood and no manufacturers beyond some skilled artisans who make individual world class furniture. The Chronicle Journal reported in an editorial on September 22, 2005 "the North still has just 70 full-time jobs making wood furniture. There are more than 40,000 such jobs in Toronto."

We have two by fours (Kenny Bucksaw sends out 10 railcar loads of 2x4's etc. from Thunder Bay every day) and we have no significant modular home units built here that could be shipped to New Orleans where a house could be erected in 24 hours. A guy in Thunder Bay wants to buy a modular home and it comes from Edmonton? The north desperately needs an entrepreneur like Kenny Bucksaw to develop value-added goods beyond just resource production.

We have world class gold mines in Red Lake, Ontario and not a goldsmith in the town. We have peat resources, wind power resources but what is the use of developing them if the power grid remains unconnected to southern Ontario and Minnesota? We have moose but no Experimental Moose Station for tourists from the USA and Europe to visit. We have the best speckled trout lakes and streams anywhere on the planet and we have no Speckled Trout Park.

There are granite quarries at Vermilion Bay, Kenora and potential quarries elsewhere in the N/NW. Where does this rock go to get cut and polished. Well, Tarana. Here we are in the Sault and Thunder Bay with cities full of good old Italian rooted boys and plenty of Scotsmen, both of whom have such a long tradition of stone masonry in their backgrounds, that they could be accused of having rocks for brains. And granite is sent to the south for finishing. How smart is that?

We have terrific tourist potential and a lack of critical mass of tourist sites for people to experience especially along Lake Superior. Ever visit the Terry Fox site outside Thunder Bay. Just how long does it take you to inspect and enjoy that memorial? I think most people would say, "half hour tops." It has no tourist retention time. There is nothing else there, no recognition of Trans Canada Fund raisers, Steve Hansen and Steve Fonyo, "The Incredible Journey" author, Sheila Burnford or Ochagac, the First Nation Chief who guided Sieur de La Verendrye and French explorers out to the west.

It is the same situation at Ouimet Canyon. It's a half hour stop. You look down take a few pictures and the kids are ready to leave. Is there a lift to the bottom of the canyon so one could experience the amazing grandeur of the place from an entirely different perspective? The only way Reeve Maria Hardwoman of Shuniah and Reeve Lindatolllady of Dorion can get to the bottom of Ouimet Canyon is to hang glide down. And speaking of Dorion, when will the Dorion Fish Hatchery get a $5 million dollar upgrade and when will the 300 or so citizens of this hamlet get their Speckled Trout Park? If they have to count on the southern Raccoons the answer might be never.

The astounding lack of business creativity in the N/NW is sad and this is keeping our wallets thin.

Nay-sayers will preach that the economics of the N/NW are so feeble it will be impossible to break with the Ontario Legislature. To this Bears say, that is like an abused partner in a marriage, who must suffer some economic pain to escape a never-ending family trauma, regardless you have to get out of the situation for the sake of your cubs and your own long term well-being. Bear Country has many resources, Bruins will reign and Bruins will survive.

The future of our cubs in the N/NW will depend upon a new assertive group of creative politicians.

ROCKY RACCOON

We have come to the end of our story with the Raccoons and the Bears. Our beloved Bear politicians will have to take it from here if they have the nerve. The future of the Bear's of the north story is in their politician's tomorrows. Perhaps the ending of Raccoon dominance of Ontarario will be the beginning of a new chapter in Canadian history. Perhaps the climax of our fable will be like the Beatle's song, Rocky Raccoon. Rocky will have lost his long abused Princess, Betty Bear and will get better from the ordeal as soon as he is able. With a Gideon's Bible in his southern Ontario room Rocky will recover and go on, and hopefully solve all the humongous issues facing he and all the other Raccoons in their very crowded domain above the lower Great lakes. Perhaps, the answer to the question, "Hey Rocky, Who Took Northern Ontario?" will be answered by:

THE BEARS TOOK IT BACK.

Hey Rocky, Who Took Northern Ontario?

END NOTES

In any story sassy enough to challenge the reactive mode of people holding political power anyone can gauge much of the response in advance. Usually, it is shoot the messenger. Forget the message and do the raccoon shuffle with a slightly faster step no matter the validity. Use something smart or smarmy to joke the content of the authors treatment as inane and ridiculous. This is one of the great facets of democracy to be able to lambaste any notion that counters the status quo. Bears say bring it on. Ideas about N/NW provincial status have been around for parts of three centuries and there is merit in trashing a political situation that fails to meet the aspirations of a free and free thinking people.

No matter what evolves here in no where Ontario it would be naive to think that there will not be an ongoing economic relationship with Tarana and the Raccoons. Come to think of it, the Raccoons and the Bears are actually members of the same forest family of critters even though most of the raccoons have moved to the city. We need corn and the Raccoons love blueberries. Trade will continue between the north and south and there is a very good chance it will actually improve with the north enfranchised as a separate province or as an extension of Manitoba.

James R. Bear
Thunder Bay, Ontario

ADDITIONAL INSANITIES

Rocky Rumsey's $4 million + "Bear Wise" Program reports a mere 28,294 calls to the toll free number at 1-866-514-2327 for 2004/05. Rocky says the phone line has "helped thousands of people learn more about bears and how to reduce bear problems." This wacky program should be entitled "How To Live With A Bear & Survive." It is an example of the continuing dysfunctional relationship between the politicians of the south and the citizens of the north. The first bear attack in the spring of 2006 was in Sudbury on a 19-year old. A small Jack Russell terrier is credited with saving the life of Matthew Facendi, not the Bear Wise Program.

Bear Folks from Makwah country keep coming and going this spring of 2006. Thunder Bay's sterile Neebing Arena recently hosted 268 evacuees Fort Albany. The day they left, 1,000 evacuees from Kashechewan head south to Geraldton, Thunder Bay, and Cochrane because spring floods and a compromised water plant mean these folks will be displaced for six to eight weeks. Bear Chief Beardy and Deputy Alvine Fiddbar have a plan. All future construction units at Fort Albany and Kashechewan will be house boats with water purifiers in the kitchens.

Calumnious column writer, Wistina Wizzard from Tarana recently asked : "How many Ontario politicians does it take to screw in a light bulb? None. Politicians don't screw in light bulbs. They screw taxpayers." To this should be added, especially northern taxpayers.

Here is some advice for the bear cubs if they have to move to Tarana for a job. (1) On hot days, they must never, absolutely never swim in Lake Ontario. (2) It will be easier to find a body piercing parlour than it will be to find a beer parlour. (3) Forget learning French as a second language in this city, Mandarin is more useful. (4) Eye contact is considered a sign of hostility there and a ruthless invasion of one's personal space, so if you feel like saying, "it's a nice day" to someone don't look at them when you say it. (5) If you are lucky enough to meet someone from Tarana be prepared to hear how all their true friends have moved to Vancouver. (6) Never talk geography with Tarana people. Anyplace beyond Oshawa is foreign to them. Tarana people need a map to find Sault Ste Marie and places beyond this are not even on earth. (7) Try and convince your cubs to move anywhere, anywhere but Tarana.

INDEX

www.ingramcontent.com/pod-product-compliance
Lightning Source LLC
Chambersburg PA
CBHW051446280526
45785CB00003B/1453